Legal Self-Help Guide

25 Estate Planning Forms

Legal Self-Help Guide

25 Estate Planning Forms

Sanket Mistry, JD, MIA, edited by J.T. Levine, JD, MFA

Peerless Legal

ISBN 13: 978-1-940788-11-1
ISBN 10: 1-940788-11-0

Mistry, Sanket
25 Estate Planning Forms: Legal Self-Help Guide
First Edition
Peerless Legal | Roanoke, Virginia | www.PeerlessLegal.com

™ and Peerless Legal are trademarks of PeerlessLegal.com.

Peerless Legal books are available for special promotions. For details, contact Peerless Legal by email at sales@peerlesslegal.com, or visit www.PeerlessLegal.com.

While the author has made every effort to provide accurate telephone numbers and internet addresses at the time of publication, neither the publisher nor author assume any responsibility for errors or changes that occur after publication. The publisher does not have any control over, and does not assume any responsibility for, author or third-party websites or their content.

This publication is designed to provide accurate and authoritative information in regard to the subject matters covered. It is sold with the understanding that the publisher and author are not engaged in rendering legal, accounting, or other professional services. If legal advice or other expert assistance is required, the services of a competent professional should be sought.

From a *Declaration of Principles jointly adopted by a Committee of the American Bar Association and a Committee of Publishers*

THIS PRODUCT IS NOT A SUBSITUTE FOR LEGAL ADVICE.
Disclaimer required by Texas statutes.

DISCLAIMER

Laws change constantly. Every effort has been made to provide the most up-to-date information. However, the author, publisher, and any and all persons or entities involved in any way in the preparation, publication, sale, or distribution of this publication disclaim any and all representations or warranties, express or implied, about the outcome or methods of use of this publication, and assume no liability for claims, losses, or damages arising from the use or misuse of this publication. All responsibilities for legal effects or consequences of any document prepared from, or action taken in reliance upon information contained in this publication are disclaimed. The reader should not rely on this author or this publisher for any professional advice. Users of this publication intending to use this publication for preparation of legal documents are advised to check specifically on the current, applicable laws in any jurisdiction in which they intend the documents to be effective. Make sure you are using the most recent edition.

Is This Legal Self-Help Guide for You?

The Peerless Legal mission is to empower individuals by giving them legal self-help tools. The Legal Self-Help Guide series was created as the embodiment of that mission.

The goal of this Guide is to provide you with the information you need to understand your legal rights and responsibilities. In doing so, we hope you will be able to resolve your legal issues yourself or know enough to feel confident in your decision to hire a licensed attorney. This Guide provides a meaningful alternative to most of the books in law libraries. Peerless Legal's goal is for you to be able to understand this material.

You are not alone in choosing self-help. Everyone faces legal issues at some point in their life. While most of us have the capacity to understand our legal rights and responsibilities, finding good legal information can be daunting. As the costs associated with legal representation rise, more and more people are opting to take certain legal matters into their own hands.

In this Guide, Peerless Legal provides you with meaningful alternatives to costly legal representation for legal issues you can handle yourself. This Guide is a plain-English alternative to the legal jargon that fills most legal books.

This book is for you if:

- you want to handle your own legal issues,
- you are not sure whether the legal issue you are facing merits the high cost of an attorney,
- you are in the process of looking for competent, legal representation, but are unsure how to evaluate legal services,
- you have retained an attorney and are unsure whether your attorney is competently handling your legal issues,
- or you want to know more about a specific legal topic.

It is important to manage expectations when acting on your own behalf or with an attorney. The forms in this book may differ from the forms that are commonly used in your local jurisdiction. You can check local rules by going to the court's website, making a phone call to the office of the clerk of court, or by visiting a local law school library. Generally, law school libraries serve as Federal repositories and are open to the public during normal business hours.

Warning There are some legal issues that seem simple and straight forward, but in reality only an attorney with extensive experience on the issue would know there is an inner-tangling.**

Dedication

For my parents who taught me love and how to strive for the best, even when the best was difficult.

Acknowledgments

This book has been nothing short of a group effort. In addition to the above named dedication, I would like to thank most J.T. Levine for her gift of editing.

About the Author

Sanket Mistry earned his JD from the Walter F. George School of Law at Mercer University. He is a member of the New York State Bar and author of several books in the Legal Self-Help Guide series. He has worked, and volunteered, at a number of nonprofits, government agencies, and for-profit corporations. He also holds a BA in philosophy from Emory University and an MIA from Columbia University. He is an avid traveler and tennis player.

About the Editor

J.T. Levine earned her JD from the Walter F. George School of Law at Mercer University. She has edited several books for Peerless Legal. She is a member of the Georgia Bar. Prior to law school, she earned an MFA in Professional Writing from the Savannah College of Art and Design and a BA from the University of Miami. She is an animal lover and has a pharaoh hound named Tut.

How to Use This Book

This book will help you get your estate in order so that you can successfully create your own legal estate documents. It includes sample forms about wills, trusts, and power of attorneys. This book is not intended to be read as a novel. It is intended to be used as a reference guide. Pay attention to headings because they are your guide-posts. This book is laid out in a way to help you find information quickly.

The forms in this book are written in plain-English with as little legal jargon as possible. However, sometimes the legal jargon cannot be avoided. Where legal jargon is used, there is, generally, a plain-English explanation that accompanies it.

By the time you finish this book, you should be able to:

- successfully understand how to, and create, your own legal documents,
- know enough about your issue to determine whether it's complicated enough to warrant hiring an attorney, and
- understand your legal rights and responsibilities.

This book contains 25 estate planning forms. Most of the content is self explanatory, but if you are unsure then you should seek resources outside of this book Not every form in this book will pertain to you or to your jurisdiction. More information about your jurisdiction is available online at the web addresses provided in the back of this book in the Appendix.

This book contains a check-list that goes along with creating a will, living trust, and powers of attorney sample legal forms. The check-lists will help you make the sample forms legal documents.

The State Specific Information at the end of the book provides links to information on each of the 50 states and the District of Columbia. Laws in different states vary and you should review this section to find your specific state rules.

The tools in this book will provide you with the most common estate planning legal form you may need to create your own estate documents or to equip you with the information you need to hire a competent attorney.

Table of Contents

Wills

Last Will and Testament Checklist

❑ Make additional copies of any specific pages you may need or tear them out of the book.

❑ Read over the blank form.

❑ If there are parts of the form you do not understand, read the applicable section within this book.

❑ Make adjustments to the form to meet your needs. If the paragraph or portion of the sample form does not apply, write "Does not apply" in the blank space.

❑ Complete the portions of the sample form with blank spaces. (Do NOT sign just yet.)

❑ If you are using this will for child(ren), but not grandchild(ren), simply put "No" in the blank space for grandchild(ren).

❑ If you are using this will for child(ren) who are NOT minors, then you can simply discard the information for guardianship and the children's trust.

❑ If you do not wish to donate your body or body parts, you can discard this part or simply write in the blank space, "I do NOT want my body, tissues, or any other part of me donated."

❑ Review the will you have completed to ensure all of the form is completed.

❑ Review the State Specific Information at PeerlessLegal.com.

❑ Meet with witnesses.

❑ Meet with Notary Public (if self-proving affidavits is desired).

❑ Double-check the will for completeness and you understand its contents.

❑ Sign and date the will in the presence of witnesses (and notary public if required or desired).

❑ If your will is complicated, or includes numerous additions, then do not use this book for the sole purpose of creating a will. Contact a licensed attorney to create a will that meets you specific needs.

❑ Give a copy of the will to the named executor and to the alternate executor.

❑ Store a record of your final, signed will, in a safe place, along with all of your other important documents that you wish to pass on.

Wills

Cover Page

Last Will and Testament

Of

_____

Date Created: _____

Notes:

LAST WILL AND TESTAMENT OF

_____

I, _____ DOB: _____,

whose address is _____

located in the County of _____ in the State of _____,

being of sound mind, willfully and voluntarily make this my Last Will and Testament ("WILL").

1. Revocation. I revoke all wills that I have previously made.

2. Marital Status. ❑ Not married ❑ Married to: _____ "SPOUSE"

3. Child(ren). ❑ No (Go to 4.) ❑ Yes, I have _____ number of child(ren):

      Name: _____ DOB: _____

      Name: _____ DOB: _____

      Name: _____ DOB: _____

      ❑ More child(ren) are listed on a separate added page dated: _____

      and titled _____.

Grandchild(ren). ❑ No (Go to 4.) ❑ Yes, I have _____number of grandchild(ren):

      Name: _____ DOB: _____

      Name: _____ DOB: _____

      Name: _____ DOB: _____

      ❑ More grandchild(ren) are listed on a separate added page dated: _____

      and titled _____.

Omissions of Child(ren) and Grandchild(ren). I do NOT leave property to one or more of the children or grandchildren omitted from the above lists of Child(ren) and Grandchild(ren); my failure to do so is intentional.

_____ My initials confirm that I have read and agreed to this term.

Personal Guardian. If, at the time of my death, any of my children are still minors, and a personal guardian is needed, I name: _____

as the "PERSONAL GUARDIAN," to serve without bond. If they are unable or unwilling to serve as Personal Guardian, I name _____ as Personal Guardian, also to serve without bond.

Property Guardian. If, at the time of my death, any of my children are minors and a property guardian is needed, I name _____

as the "PROPERTY GUARDIAN," to serve without bond. If they are unable or unwilling to serve as Property Guardian, I name _____

as Property Guardian, also to serve without bond.

Children's Trust. Property left in this Will to beneficiaries listed in Section A (below in this Section) is held in a separate trust, administered according to the following terms:

> **A. Trust Beneficiaries and Age Limits.** Each trust ends when the following beneficiaries become 35 years of age, except as otherwise specified in this section.

> Trust Beneficiary (Name)   Trust Ends at Age

> _____   _____

> _____   _____

> _____   _____

> **B. Trustees.** I name _____"TRUSTEE," to serve without bond. If they are unable or unwilling to serve as Trustee, I name _____ _____as Trustee, also to serve without bond.

> **C. Beneficiary Provisions.**

> (1) Trustee may distribute for the benefit of each beneficiary as much of the net income or principal of the trust as the Trustee deems necessary for the beneficiary's health, support, maintenance, and education. In deciding whether to make a distribution for or to a beneficiary, the Trustee may take into account the beneficiary's other income, resources, and sources of support.

> (2) Any trust income that is not distributed to a beneficiary by the Trustee will accumulate and will be added to the principal of the trust administered for that beneficiary.

> **D. Termination of Trust.** The trust terminates if and when any of the following occurs:

(A) beneficiary becomes the age specified in Paragraph A of this trust;

(B) beneficiary dies before becoming the age specified in Paragraph A of this trust; or

(C) trust property is used up through distributions allowed under these provisions.

If the trust is terminated due to the beneficiary reaching the age specified in Paragraph A of this trust, the remaining principal and accumulated net income of the trust passes to the trust beneficiary.

If the trust is terminated due to the beneficiary's death, the remaining principal and accumulated net income in the trust passes to the deceased trust beneficiary's heirs.

E. Powers of Trustee. In addition to other powers granted to the Trustee in this Will, the Trustee has the powers:

(1) generally conferred on trustees by the laws of the state having jurisdiction over this trust;

(2) with respect to property in the trust, conferred by this Will on the Executor; and

(3) to hire and pay from trust assets the reasonable fees of investment advisors, accountants, tax advisors, agents, attorneys, and other assistants to administer the trust and manage any trust asset and for any litigation affecting the trust.

F. Trust Administration Provisions.

(1) This trust is to be administered independent of court supervision to the maximum extent possible under the laws of the state having jurisdiction over this trust.

(2) The interests of trust beneficiaries are not transferable by voluntary or involuntary assignment or by operation of law and be free from the claims of creditors and from attachment, execution, bankruptcy or other legal process to the fullest extent permissible by law.

(3) The trustee is entitled to reasonable compensation out of the trust assets for ordinary and extraordinary services, and for all services in connection with the complete or partial termination of any trust created by this Will.

(4) The invalidity of any provision of this trust instrument does not affect the validity of the remaining provisions.

4. Beneficiary Survival Requirement. Beneficiaries named in this Will must survive me by at least thirty (30) calendar days to receive any property under this Will.

5. Simultaneous Death. If any beneficiary and I die simultaneously (in the same transaction and/or occurrence within twenty-nine (29) calendar days from one another), for purposes of this Will, I am presumed to have survived the beneficiary.

6. Define: Survive. In this Will, "survive" means to outlive the will writer by at least forty-five (45) calendar days ("SURVIVE").

7. Specific Gifts. All specific gifts made in this Will to two or more beneficiaries, receive equal interest in the specific gifts, unless unequal shares are specifically indicated. All shared gifts are required to be sold with the net proceeds distributed as directed by this Will, unless all beneficiaries of the gift agree in writing, after the Will creator's death, that the specific gift is not be sold.

If I name two or more primary beneficiaries to receive a specific gift of property and any of the primary beneficiaries does not survive me, then all of the surviving primary beneficiaries receive, in equal shares, the interest in the non-surviving, deceased, primary beneficiary's share (i.e., the last in time surviving, primary beneficiaries take possession of the specific gift with the non-surviving beneficiary's share distributed equally among the remaining, surviving, beneficiaries and no effect on the surviving primary beneficiaries' initial interest), unless I have specifically provided otherwise. If I name two or more alternate beneficiaries to receive a specific gift of property, and any of them do not survive me, all surviving, alternate beneficiaries are to equally divide the deceased, alternate beneficiary's share.

I make the following specific gifts of property that are detailed in **Schedule A. Schedule A** is a part of this Will.

8. Residuary Estate. The remaining property not named or disposed of by this Will, or any other manner, including lapsed or failed gifts, is included as part of my residuary estate, which goes:

(My initials are provided next to my **one** selection for the residuary beneficiary of this Will.)

_____ to my Spouse, or if my Spouse does not survive me, alternatively, then to my child(ren): _____, and alternatively, if they do not survive me, then to: _____ _____.

[OR]

_____ to: _____,

and alternatively, if they do not survive me, then to: _____

_____.

If I name two or more alternate residuary beneficiaries to receive property and any of them do not survive me, all surviving alternate residuary beneficiaries are to equally divide the deceased alternate residuary beneficiary's share.

9. Executor. I name _____, "EXECUTOR," to serve

without bond; however, if not qualified, or ceases to serve, then I name _____

_____ as the alternate Executor, who also will serve without bond.

My Executor is directed to take all legal actions to probate this Will, including filing a petition in the proper court for the independent administration of my estate.

The location of all of my documents to be distributed by this Will is: _____

_____.

I grant to my Executor the following powers, to be exercised as the Executor deems in the best interest of my estate, to:

(1) retain property, without liability for loss or depreciation resulting from such retention.

(2) sell, lease, or exchange property and to receive or administer the proceeds as a part of my estate.

(3) vote stock, convert bonds, notes, stocks or other securities belonging to my estate into other securities, and exercise all other rights and privileges of a person owning similar property.

(4) deal with, and settle, claims in favor of or against my estate.

(5) continue, maintain, operate or participate in any business which is a part of my estate, and to incorporate, dissolve or otherwise change the form of organization of the business.

(6) pay all debts and taxes that may be assessed against my estate, as provided under state law.

(7) do all other acts which, in the executor's judgment, may be necessary or appropriate for the proper and advantageous management, investment, and distribution of my estate.

These powers, authority, and discretion are in addition to the powers, authority, and discretion vested in an Executor by operation of law, and may be exercised as often as deemed necessary, without approval by any court in any jurisdiction.

10. Anatomical Gift. I declare, under the Uniform Anatomical Gift Act, to donate to any medical institution willing to accept and use them, and I direct my Executor to carry out such donation of the following body parts and organs: _____

_____

_____

11. Funeral Arrangements. Funeral arrangements have been made with the _____

_____ located at _____

_____

to be buried at _____

located in _____

and I direct my Executor to carry out such arrangements.

I sign my name to this Will this _____ day of _____, 20_____, at

_____, in the State of _____, and declare it is my Will, that I sign willingly, execute freely and voluntarily for the purposes expressed, that I am of the age of majority or otherwise legally empowered to make a Will, and under no constraint or undue influence.

_____   _____
Signature of Testator   Printed Name of Testator

WITNESS STATEMENT

On this _____ day of _____, 20_____, the Testator, _____ declared to us, the undersigned, that this instrument is Testator's Will. Testator requests us to act as witnesses. Testator has signed this Will in our presence, all of us being present at the same time. We now, at the Testator's request, in the Testator's presence, and in the presence of each other, sign and print our names as witnesses to declare that we are of sound mind and of proper age to act as witnesses to a will. We further declare that we understand this to be the Testator's Will, and that, to the best of our knowledge, the Testator is of the legal age, or is otherwise legally empowered to make a will, and appears to be of sound mind and under no constraint or undue influence.

We declare, under penalty of perjury of law, that the above declaration is true and correct, this

_____ day of _____, 20 _____, at _____, located in

the County of _____ in the State of _____.

_____   _____
Witness's Signature   Printed Name of Witness
_____
Address of Witness

_____   _____
Witness's Signature   Printed Name of Witness
_____
Address of Witness

_____   _____
Witness's Signature   Printed Name of Witness
_____
Address of Witness

SCHEDULE A—Specific Gifts.

I make the following specific gifts of property: I leave _____

described as _____

_____

to _____

and, alternatively, if they do not survive me, then to _____

_____

I make the following specific gifts of property: I leave _____

described as _____

_____

to _____

and, alternatively, if they do not survive me, then to _____

_____

I make the following specific gifts of property: I leave _____

described as _____

_____

to _____

and, alternatively, if they do not survive me, then to _____

_____

I make the following specific gifts of property: I leave _____

described as _____

_____

to _____

and, alternatively, if they do not survive me, then to _____

_____

One entry per item.   **Last Will and Testament**   Page _____ of _____
Copy as needed.

Wills

Cover Page

Self-Proving Affidavit

Of

_____

Date Created: _____

Notes:

SELF-PROVING AFFIDAVIT 1: Alabama, Alaska, Arizona, Arkansas, Colorado, Connecticut, Hawaii, Idaho, Illinois, Indiana, Maine, Michigan, Minnesota, Mississippi, Montana, Nebraska, Nevada, New Mexico, New York, North Dakota, Oregon, South Carolina, South Dakota, Tennessee, Utah, Virginia, Washington (State), West Virginia, or Wisconsin

We, _____, _____

_____and _____,
the testator and the witnesses, whose names are signed to the attached instrument in those capacities, personally appearing before the undersigned authority and being first duly sworn, declare to the undersigned authority under penalty of perjury that:

(1) the testator declared, signed, and executed the instrument as his or her last will;

(2) he or she signed it willingly or directed another to sign for him or her;

(3) he or she executed it as his or her free and voluntary act for the purposes therein expressed; and

(4) each of the witnesses, at the request of the testator, in his or her hearing and presence and in the presence of each other, signed the will as witnesses, and that to the best of his or her knowledge the testator was at that time of full legal age, of sound mind and under no constraint or undue influence.

Testator's Signature: _____

_____   _____
Witness's Signature   Printed Name of Witness

_____
Address of Witness

_____   _____
Witness's Signature   Printed Name of Witness

_____
Address of Witness

_____   _____
Witness's Signature   Printed Name of Witness

_____
Address of Witness

NOTARY PUBLIC ACKNOWLEDGEMENT

The foregoing instrument was acknowledged, subscribed, and sworn to before me, this _____ day of _____, 20_____, by _____, the testator, and by _____, _____, and _____, personally known to me (or proved to me on the basis of satisfactory evidence) to be the person whose name is subscribed to the foregoing instrument, and acknowledged to me that he or she executed the same in his or her authorized capacity and that by his or her signature on the instrument, the person, or the entity upon behalf of which the person acted, executed the instrument.

Witness my hand and official seal.

_____

NOTARY PUBLIC for the State of _____

My Commission Expires: _____

[For Notary Seal or Stamp]

_____
NOTARY PUBLIC

Wills

Cover Page

Self-Proving Affidavit

Of

_____

Date Created: _____

Notes:

SELF-PROVING AFFIDAVIT 2: Delaware, Florida, Georgia, Iowa, Kansas, Kentucky, Massachusetts, Missouri, New Jersey, North Carolina, Oklahoma, Pennsylvania, Rhode Island, or Wyoming

We, _____, _____,

_____and_____
the witnesses, whose names are signed to the attached or foregoing instrument and whose signatures appear below, having appeared together before me and having been first duly sworn, each then declared to me that:

1) the attached or foregoing instrument is the last will of the testator;

2) the testator willingly and voluntarily declared, signed and executed the will in the presence of the witnesses;

3) the witnesses signed the will upon request by the testator, in the presence and hearing of the testator and in the presence of each other;

4) to the best knowledge of each witness the testator was, at that time of the signing, of the age of majority (or otherwise legally competent to make a will), of sound mind and under no constraint or undue influence; and

5) each witness was and is competent, and of the proper age to witness a will.

Testator's Signature: _____

_____   _____
Witness's Signature   Printed Name of Witness

_____
Address of Witness

_____   _____
Witness's Signature   Printed Name of Witness

_____
Address of Witness

_____   _____
Witness's Signature   Printed Name of Witness

_____
Address of Witness

NOTARY PUBLIC ACKNOWLEDGEMENT

The foregoing instrument was acknowledged, subscribed, and sworn to before me, this _____ day

of _____, 20_____, by _____, the testator, and

by _____, _____,

and _____, personally known to me (or proved to me on the basis of satisfactory evidence) to be the person whose name is subscribed to the foregoing instrument, and acknowledged to me that he or she executed the same in his or her authorized capacity and that by his or her signature on the instrument, the person, or the entity upon behalf of which the person acted, executed the instrument.

Witness my hand and official seal.

_____

NOTARY PUBLIC for the State of _____

My Commission Expires: _____

[For Notary Seal or Stamp]

_____
NOTARY PUBLIC

Cover Page

Self-Proving Affidavit

Of

_____

Date Created: _____

Notes:

SELF-PROVING AFFIDAVIT TEXAS

THE STATE OF TEXAS, COUNTY OF _____.

Before me, the undersigned authority, on this day personally appeared _____,

_____, _____,

and _____, known to me (or proved to me on the basis of satisfactory evidence) to be the testator and the witnesses, respectively, whose names are subscribed on the foregoing instrument, and, all have been duly sworn by me. The testator declared to me and to the witnesses in my presence that the foregoing instrument is their last will and testament, and that the testator willingly made and executed it as a free act. The witnesses, each on their oath stated to me, in the presence and hearing of the testator, that the testator declared to them that the instrument is the testator's last will and testament, and that the testator executed it and wanted each of them to sign as witnesses. On the witnesses' oaths, each witness stated further that all of the witnesses signed the instrument as witnesses in the presence of the testator at the testator's request, and that the testator was at the time eighteen years of age or over (or being under such age, was or had been lawfully married, or was then a member of the armed forces of the United States or an auxiliary thereof or of the Maritime Service) and was of sound mind, and each witness was then at least fourteen years of age.

Testator's Signature: _____

_____ _____
Witness's Signature   Printed Name of Witness

_____ _____
Witness's Signature   Printed Name of Witness

_____ _____
Witness's Signature   Printed Name of Witness

NOTARY PUBLIC ACKNOWLEDGEMENT

The foregoing instrument was acknowledged, subscribed, and sworn to before me, this _____day of _____, 20_____.

Witness my hand and official seal. _____

NOTARY PUBLIC for the State of _____My Commission Expires: _____

[For Notary Seal or Stamp]

_____
NOTARY PUBLIC

Wills

Cover Page

Living Will

Of

_____

Date Created: _____

Notes:

LIVING WILL OF _____

I, _____ (DOB: _____), whose address

is _____ in the County of _____

in the State of _____ , ("PRINCIPAL") being of sound mind, willfully, and voluntarily make this, my Living Will, if I become incompetent or incapacitated to the extent that I am unable to communicate my wishes, desires, and preferences on my own regarding my healthcare. This declaration is an expression of my legal right to refuse healthcare and treatment, and my life is not to be artificially prolonged under the circumstances set forth below, and, pursuant to any and all applicable laws in the State of _____ .

I revoke all Living Wills that I have previously made.

I expect, and trust, all parties involved in my healthcare needs to be legally and morally bound to act in accordance with my wishes, desires, and preferences in this document. I declare:

(By placing my initials before each number means I grant those powers, and where there are no initials means I do NOT grant those powers. I may also cross out powers which are NOT granted. Where there are letters as subparts to the numbers, I place my initials next to the numbers and letters to confirm the grant of the specific powers. Each of the letters that have been agreed to, are initialed. No initial next to a letter, means the power is not granted to that part.)

_____ 1. **Terminal Condition.** If I should have an incurable or irreversible condition which has been certified as a terminal condition that will cause my death within a relatively short time by my attending physician and one additional physician, both of whom have personally examined me, and such physicians have determined that there can be no recovery from such condition and my death is imminent, and where the application of life prolonging procedures would serve only to artificially prolong the dying process, and are not necessary to my comfort, care, or to alleviate pain, then this authorization includes, but is not limited to, the **withholding or the withdrawal of the following types of medical treatment** (subject to any special instructions in Paragraph 7 below):

_____ a. Artificial feeding and hydration.

_____ b. Cardiopulmonary resuscitation (this includes, but is not limited to, the use of drugs, electric shock, and artificial breathing).

_____ c. Kidney dialysis.

_____ d. Surgery or other invasive procedures.

_____ e. Drugs and antibiotics.

_____ f. Transfusions of blood or blood products.

_____ g. Other: _____

_____.

_____ 2. **Irreversible Coma or Persistent Vegetative State.** If I should be in an irreversible coma or persistent vegetative state which has been certified as incurable by my attending physician and one additional physician, both of whom have personally examined me, and such physicians have determined that there can be no recovery from such condition and my death is imminent, and where the application of life prolonging procedures would serve only to artificially prolong the dying process, and are not necessary to my comfort, care, or to alleviate pain, then this authorization includes, but is not limited to, the **withholding or the withdrawal of the following types of medical treatment** (subject to any special instructions in Paragraph 7 below):

_____ a. Artificial feeding and hydration.

_____ b. Cardiopulmonary resuscitation (this includes, but is not limited to, the use of drugs, electric shock, and artificial breathing).

_____ c. Kidney dialysis.

_____ d. Surgery or other invasive procedures.

_____ e. Drugs and antibiotics.

_____ f. Transfusions of blood or blood products.

_____ g. Other: _____

_____.

_____ 3. **Medical Condition Where I Cannot Communicate.** If I have a medical condition where I am unable to communicate my desires as to treatment, and my physician determines that the burdens of treatment outweigh the expected benefits, I direct my attending physician to withhold or withdraw medical procedures and treatment other than the medical procedures and treatment necessary for my comfort or to alleviate pain. This authorization includes, but is not limited to, the **withholding or withdrawal of the following types of medical treatment** (subject to any special instructions in paragraph 7 below):

_____ a. Artificial feeding and hydration.

_____ b. Cardiopulmonary resuscitation (this includes, but is not limited to, the use of drugs, electric shock, and artificial breathing).

_____ c. Kidney dialysis.

_____ d. Surgery or other invasive procedures.

_____ e. Drugs and antibiotics.

_____ f. Transfusions of blood or blood products.

_____ g. Other: _____

_____.

_____ 4. **Life Prolonged.** I want my life prolonged to the greatest extent possible (subject to any special instructions in paragraph 7 below).

_____ 5. **Pregnancy.** If I am diagnosed as pregnant, this document shall have no force and effect during my pregnancy.

_____ 6. **Durable Power of Attorney for Healthcare.** If I have also signed a Durable Power of Attorney for Healthcare, Appointment of Healthcare Agent, or Healthcare Proxy, I direct the person who I have appointed with such instrument to follow the directions that I have made in this document.

_____ 7. **Additional Directions.** I have the following additional directions: _____

_____

_____.

_____ 8. **Limitations on Decision-Makers.** I DO NOT want the following person(s) to be involved in any manner in the decision-making regarding my medical treatment, or the withholding or withdrawal of medical treatment: _____

_____

_____.

I understand the full importance of this declaration, and I am emotionally and mentally competent to make this declaration and Living Will. I also understand that I may revoke this document at any time. I publish and sign this Living Will on this ____day of _____, 20____, and declare that I do so freely, for the purposes expressed, under no constraint or undue influence, and that I am of sound mind and of legal age.

Principal's Signature: _____

WITNESS STATEMENT

On this _____ day of _____, 20_____, the Principal, _____

_____ declared to us, the undersigned, that this instrument is the Principal's Living Will. Principal has signed this Living Will in our presence, all of us being present at the same time. We now, at the Principal's request, in the Principal's presence, and in the presence of each other, sign and print our names as witnesses to declare that we are of sound mind and of proper age to act as witnesses to a living will. We further declare that to the best of our knowledge the Principal is of the legal age, or is otherwise legally empowered to make a living will, and appears to be of sound mind and under no constraint or undue influence. We are not the Principal's attending physician, or a patient or employee of the Principal's attending physi-cian; or a patient, physician, or employee of the healthcare facility in which the Principal is a patient, unless such person is required or allowed to witness the execution of this document by the laws of the state in which this document is executed. We also are not entitled to any portion of the Principal's estate on the Principal's death under the laws of intestate succession of any state, or under the Last Will and Testament of the Principal or any Codicil to such Last Will and Testament, and not directly financially responsible for the Principal's medical care. We further did not sign the Principal's signature for the Principal or on the direction of the Principal, nor have we been paid any fee for acting as witnesses to the execution of this document.

We declare, under penalty of perjury of law, that the above declaration is true and correct, this

_____ day of _____, 20 _____, at _____, located in

the County of _____ in the State of _____.

_____   _____
Witness's Signature   Printed Name of Witness
_____
Address of Witness

_____   _____
Witness's Signature   Printed Name of Witness
_____
Address of Witness

_____   _____
Witness's Signature   Printed Name of Witness
_____
Address of Witness

NOTARY PUBLIC ACKNOWLEDGEMENT

The foregoing instrument was acknowledged, subscribed, and sworn to before me, this ____day

of _____, 20_____, by _____, the Principal,

and by _____, _____,

and _____, personally known to me (or proved to me on the basis of satisfactory evidence) to be the person whose name is subscribed to the foregoing instrument, and acknowledged to me that he or she executed the same in his or her authorized capacity and that by his or her signature on the instrument, the person, or the entity upon behalf of which the person acted, executed the instrument.

Witness my hand and official seal.

_____

NOTARY PUBLIC for the State of _____

My Commission Expires: _____

[For Notary Seal or Stamp]

_____

NOTARY PUBLIC

Wills

Cover Page

Will Amendment

Of

_____

Date Created: _____

Notes:

WILL AMENDMENT

I, _____(DOB:_____), whose address

is _____in the County of _____

in the State of _____, declare that this is an amendment to my Will that is dated:

_____.

1) I make the following changes: _____

_____

_____

_____

_____

_____

_____

2) I add the following to my Will: _____

_____

_____

_____

_____

_____

_____

_____

3) In all other respects, I confirm and republish my Will dated _____
as modified by this amendment.

I subscribe my name to this amendment this day of _____, 20____, at _____, located in the County of _____ in the State of _____

and I declare, under penalty of perjury of the law, that I am signing and executing this amendment willingly, under my own free and voluntary act, and that I am of the age of majority or otherwise legally empowered to make an amendment, and I am under no constraint or undue influence.

_____
Signature

WITNESS STATEMENT

On this _____ day of _____, 20_____, the Testator, _____, declared to us, the undersigned, that this instrument is Testator's amendment. Testator requests us to act as witnesses. Testator has signed this amendment in our presence, all of us being present at the same time. We now, at the Testator's request, in the Testator's presence, and in the presence of each other, sign and print our names as witnesses to declare that we are of sound mind and of proper age to act as witnesses to an amendment to a will. We further declare that we understand this to be the Testator's amendment, and that to the best of our knowledge the Testator is of the legal age, or is otherwise legally empowered to make an amendment and will, and appears to be of sound mind and under no constraint or undue influence.

We declare, under penalty of perjury of law, that the above declaration is true and correct, this

_____ day of _____, 20_____, at _____, located in the County of _____ in the State of _____.

_____
Witness's Signature

_____
Printed Name of Witness

_____
Address of Witness

_____
Witness's Signature

_____
Printed Name of Witness

_____
Address of Witness

_____
Witness's Signature

_____
Printed Name of Witness

_____
Address of Witness

Wills

Cover Page

Will Revocation

Of

_____

Date Created: _____

Notes:

WILL REVOCATION

I, _____(DOB:_____), whose address

is _____in the County of _____

in the State of _____, revoke the my Will dated: _____, and

titled _____in its entirety without

limitations, including revoking any appointment of any persons named in the above Will.

Revoking party's signature: _____Date: _____

NOTARY PUBLIC ACKNOWLEDGEMENT

The foregoing instrument was acknowledged, subscribed, and sworn to before me,

_____this _____day of _____,

20_____, personally known to me (or proved to me on the basis of satisfactory evidence) to be the person whose name is subscribed to the foregoing instrument, and acknowledged to me that he or she executed the same in his or her authorized capacity and that by his or her signature on the instrument, the person, or the entity upon behalf of which the person acted, executed the instrument.

Witness my hand and official seal.

NOTARY PUBLIC for the State of _____, County of _____

My Commission Expires: _____

[For Notary Seal or Stamp]

Wills

Cover Page

Ethical Will

Of

_____

Date Created: _____

Notes:

Ethical Will

From: _____

_____

_____

Date: _____

To: _____

_____

_____

I write this letter, my ethical will, to you now, in the hopes that in reading this will provide you strength, and the chance to remember me. In creating this ethical will, I share with you some wisdom I have acquired over my life about love, happiness, and my dreams. I hope you will feel my love for you through this letter.

First, I love you! _____

_____

_____

I believe that we never truly loose the people we love. _____

_____

_____

The message I leave to you is that I have lived, loved, and found peace. _____

_____

_____

I have lived. _____

_____

_____

I have loved. _____

_____

_____

I have found peace. _____

_____

_____

What I value: _____

_____

What I believe in: _____

_____

Lessons I have learned. _____

_____

_____

You have meant so much to me. _____

_____

I leave you with these thoughts. _____

_____

_____

My last wishes are: _____

_____

_____

We will see each other again. _____

_____

My final thoughts are with you. _____

_____

Love: _____

Cover Page

Explanation Letter

Of

_____

Date Created: _____

Notes:

Explanation Letter

From: _____

_____

_____

Date: _____

To: _____

_____

_____

I write this letter, in order to provide you with some explanation and clarity for why I have made certain decisions in my will. I hope this will help to avoid any prolonged disputes about the contents of my will and estate.

I intentionally left unequal shares of: _____.

By doing this, I hope to achieve: _____

_____.

I intentionally left unequal shares of: _____.

By doing this, I hope to achieve: _____

_____.

I intentionally left unequal shares of: _____.

By doing this, I hope to achieve: _____

_____.

I intentionally left unequal shares of: _____.

By doing this, I hope to achieve: _____

_____.

Signature: _____   Date: _____

Power of Attorney

Power of Attorney Checklist

❑ Make additional copies of any specific pages you may need or tear them out of the book.

❑ Read over the blank form.

❑ If there are parts of the form you do not understand, read the applicable section within this book.

❑ Make adjustments to the form to meet your needs. If the paragraph or portion of the sample form does not apply, write "Does not apply" in the blank space.

❑ Complete the portions of the sample form with blank spaces. (Do NOT sign just yet.)

❑ Review the Power of Attorney you have completed to ensure all of the form is completed.

❑ Review the State Specific Information at PeerlessLegal.com.

❑ Meet with witnesses and with the Notary Public.

❑ Make sure that you the information you have provided is complete and that you understand what is contained within the Power of Attorney.

❑ Sign and date the Power of Attorney in the presence of the witnesses and Notary Public.

❑ If your Power of Attorney is complicated or includes numerous additions, then do not use this book or its contents for the sole purpose of creating a Power of Attorney. Contact a licensed attorney to help you create a Power of Attorney that meets your specific needs.

❑ Give a copy of the complete Power of Attorney to the named Agent and to the alternative Agent.

❑ Store the completed Power of Attorney in a safe place, along with all other important documents that you wish to pass on.

Power of Attorney

Cover Page

Durable Power of Attorney for Healthcare

Of

_____

Date Created: _____

Notes:

DURABLE POWER OF ATTORNEY FOR HEALTHCARE

I, _____(DOB:_____) whose address

is _____in the County of _____

in the State of _____, appoint _____,

who resides at _____

as my agent for healthcare and related personal decisions for me except as I provide otherwise in this document ("AGENT"). If my Agent is unable or unwilling to make those decisions, I appoint as an alternate Agent _____, residing

at _____.

I grant my Agent the maximum power allowed under the law to perform any acts, or make any decisions, on my behalf regarding healthcare matters that I could do, or make, personally, under the laws of the State of _____, including making healthcare decisions on my behalf under the terms and conditions set forth below. My Agent accepts this appointment and agrees to act in my best interest as my Agent considers advisable. This Durable Power of Attorney for Healthcare may be revoked, by me, at any time, and is automatically revoked upon my death.

I revoke all Durable Power of Attorney for Healthcare that I have previously made.

I specifically DO NOT want the following person(s) to be involved, in any manner, in the decision-making regarding my medical treatment, or the withholding or withdrawal of medical treatment: _____

_____.

This Durable Power of Attorney for Healthcare has the following terms and conditions:

1. Superior Document. If I have signed a Living Will or a Directive to Physicians that is valid, then I direct my Agent to follow the directions set out in that document.

2. Terminal Condition Diagnosis. If, at any time, I am diagnosed as having an incurable injury, disease, or illness, which has been certified as a terminal condition by my attending physician and one additional physician, both of which have personally examined me, and such physicians have determined that there can be no recovery from such a condition, and where the application of life prolonging procedures would only serve to artificially prolong the dying process, then:

> I direct my Agent to withhold or withdraw such procedures, and that I may be permitted to die naturally, with only the administration of medication, the administration of

nutrition and/or hydration, or the performance of any medical procedure deemed necessary to provide comfort, care, or to alleviate pain.

3. Persistent Vegetative State Diagnosis. If, at any time, I am diagnosed as being in a persistent, vegetative state, which has been certi-fied as incurable by my attending physician and one additional physician after both have personally examined me, and such physicians have determined that there can be no recovery from such a condition, and where the application of life prolonging procedures would serve only to artificially prolong the dying process, then:

> I direct that my Agent should withhold or withdraw such procedures, and that I be permitted to die naturally with only the administration of medication, the administration of nutrition and/or hydration, or the performance of any medical procedure deemed necessary to provide me with comfort, care, or to alleviate pain.

4. Effective Date and Durability. My Agent may only act if I am unable to participate in making decisions regarding my medical treatment. My attending physician and another physician or licensed psychologist must determine, after examining me, whether I am unable to participate in making my own medical decisions. This designation is suspended during any period when I regain the ability to participate in my own medical treatment decisions. I intend this document to be a Durable Power of Attorney for Healthcare and to survive my disability or incapacity. If I am able to communicate in any manner, including even blinking my eyes, I direct that my healthcare representative try and discuss with me the specifics of any proposed healthcare decision.

5. Agent's Powers. I grant my Agent full authority to make decisions for me. In making such decisions, the Agent must follow my expressed wishes, either written or oral, regarding my medical treatment. If my Agent cannot determine the choice I would want, based on my written or oral statements, then my Agent is to choose for me based on what my Agent believes to be in my best interest. I direct that my Agent comply with the following instructions or limitations:

_____

_____

_____.

I have discussed my healthcare wishes with my Agent and I am satisfied that my Agent knows my wishes with respect to my healthcare and I have full faith and confidence in their judgment. I further direct that my Agent have full authority to do the following, should I lack the capacity to make such a decision myself, provided, however, that this listing is construed in no way to limit the full authority I give my Agent to make healthcare decisions on my behalf to:

> a. give informed consent to any healthcare procedure;

b. sign documents necessary to carry out, or withhold, any healthcare procedures on my behalf, including any waivers or releases of liabilities required by any healthcare provider;

c. give or withhold consent for any healthcare or treatment;

d. revoke or change any consent previously given, or implied by law for any healthcare treatment;

e. arrange for, or authorize, my placement or removal from any healthcare facility or institution;

f. require any procedures be discontinued; including the withholding of any medical treatment and/or aid, including nutrition, hydration, and any other medical procedure deemed necessary to provide comfort, care, or to alleviate pain, subject to the conditions previously provided in this docu-ment;

g. authorize the administration of pain-relieving drugs, even if they may shorten my life.

I wish for all my healthcare matters to be carried out through the authority that I have provided to my Agent in this document, despite any contrary wishes, beliefs, or opinions of any members of my family, relatives, or friends.

6. Life-Sustaining Treatment. (CHOOSE <u>ONLY</u> ONE OR NONE of the three.) I understand that I do not have to choose any of the instructions regarding life-sustaining treatment listed below. If I choose one, I will place a mark by the choice and sign below my choice. If I sign one of the choices listed below, I direct that reasonable measures be taken to keep me comfortable and to relieve pain.

❑   <u>CHOICE 1</u>: Life-sustaining treatment: I grant discretion to my Agent.

I do not want life-sustaining treatment (❑ including artificial delivery of food and water ❑ except for artificial delivery of food and water) if any of the following medical conditions exist:

a. I am in an irreversible coma or persistent vegetative state.

b. I am terminally ill, and life-sustaining procedures would only serve to artificially delay my death.

c. My medical condition is such that the burdens of treatment outweigh the expected benefits. In making this determination, I want my Patient Advocate to consider relief of my suffering, the expenses involved, and the quality of life, if prolonged.

I expressly authorize my Agent to make decisions to withhold or withdraw treatment which would allow me to die, and I acknowledge such decisions could or would result in my death.

Signed: _____

[OR]

❏   <u>CHOICE 2</u>: Life-sustaining treatment: I authorize my Agent to withhold all medical treatment if I am ever in a coma or in a persistent, vegetative state.

I want life-sustaining treatment (❏ including artificial delivery of food and water ❏ except for artificial delivery of food and water) unless I am in a coma or persistent vegetative state that my physician reasonably believes to be irreversible. Once my physician has reasonably concluded that I will remain unconscious for the rest of my life, I do not want life-sustaining treatment to be provided or continued.

I expressly authorize my Agent to make decisions to withhold or withdraw treatment which would allow me to die, and I acknowledge such decisions could or would result in my death.

Signed: _____

[OR]

❏   <u>CHOICE 3</u>: Directive for maximum treatment.

I want my life to be prolonged to the greatest extent possible consistent with sound medical practice without regard to my condition, the chances I have for recovery, or the cost of the procedures, and I direct life-sustaining treatment to be provided in order to prolong my life.

Signed: _____

7. If No Agent. If I am unable to participate in making decisions for my care, and there is no Agent to act for me, I request for the instructions I have given in this document to be followed and that those instructions will be considered conclusive evidence of my wishes.

8. Administrative Provisions. I revoke any prior durable powers of attorney for healthcare that I may have executed to the extent that they grant powers and authority within the scope of the powers granted to the Agent appointed in this document.

Photocopies of this signed, power of attorney shall be treated as original counterparts.

9. Duration. This Durable Power of Attorney for Healthcare exists, indefinitely, from its date of execution, until I revoke it.

I am providing these instructions voluntarily, I am at least eighteen years old, and of sound mind.

Date: _____ Signature: _____

WITNESS STATEMENT

On this _____day of _____, 20_____, we, _____

and _____, declare under penalty of perjury that the person who signed or acknowledged this document is personally known to me (or proved to me on the basis of convincing evidence) to be the principal, that the principal signed or acknowledged this durable power of attorney for healthcare in my presence, that the principal appears to be of sound mind and under no duress, fraud, or undue influence. We are not appointed as Agent by this document. We are not related to the principal by blood, marriage, or adoption. We would not be entitled to any portion of the principal's estate upon the principal's death. We are not the attending physician of the principal or an employee of the attending physician. We have no claim against any portion of the principal's estate upon the principal's death. Furthermore, if we are an employee of a healthcare facility in which the principal is a patient, we are not involved in providing direct patient care to the principal and not one of us is an officer, director, partner, or business office employee of the healthcare facility or of any parent organization of the healthcare facility.

_____   _____
Witness's Signature   Printed Name of Witness

_____
Address of Witness

_____   _____
Witness's Signature   Printed Name of Witness

_____
Address of Witness

NOTARY PUBLIC ACKNOWLEDGEMENT

The foregoing instrument was acknowledged, subscribed, and sworn to before me, this _____ day

of _____, 20_____, by _____, and witnessed

by _____, and _____,
personally known to me (or proved to me on the basis of satisfactory evidence) to be the person whose name is subscribed to the foregoing instrument, and acknowledged to me that he or she executed the same in his or her authorized capacity and that by his or her signature on the instrument, the person, or the entity upon behalf of which the person acted, executed the instrument.

Witness my hand and official seal.

_____

NOTARY PUBLIC for the State of _____

My Commission Expires: _____

[For Notary Seal or Stamp]

_____
NOTARY PUBLIC

Power of Attorney

Cover Page

Financial Durable Power of Attorney

Of

_____

Date Created: _____

Notes:

FINANCIAL DURABLE POWER OF ATTORNEY

I, _____(DOB: _____), whose address

is _____in the County of _____

in the State of _____,"PRINCIPAL," appoint _____,

whose address is_____

as my Power of Attorney for financial and related decisions for me, except as I provide otherwise in this document ("AGENT"). If my Agent is unable or unwilling to make those decisions, I

appoint, as an alternate Agent, _____, whose address

is _____.

I grant my Agent the maximum power allowed under the law to perform any acts on my behalf regarding financial matters that I could do personally under the laws of the State of _____ _____, on my behalf under the terms and conditions below. My Agent will act as my attorney-in-fact to act in my name, place, and stead in any way which I myself could do with respect to the matters in this document, to the extent that I am permitted by law to act through an Agent. My Agent accepts this appointment and agrees to act in my best interest as my Agent considers advisable.

By placing my initials before one selection below means I grant those powers of attorney to my Agent. Where there are no initials means I do NOT grant those powers of attorney to my Agent.

_____   **THIS FINANCIAL DURABLE POWER OF ATTORNEY IS EFFECTIVE IMMEDIATELY.**

[OR]

_____   **THIS FINANCIAL DURABLE POWER OF ATTORNEY IS ONLY EFFECTIVE IF I BECOME PERMANENTLY DISABILITY OR INCAPACITATED, WHICH HAS BEEN CERTIFIED AS INCURABLE BY MY ATTENDING PHYSICIAN AND ONE ADDITIONAL PHYSICAN, BOTH OF WHOM HAVE PERSONALLY EXAMINED ME, AND SUCH PHYSICIANS HAVE DETERMINED THAT THERE CAN BE NO RECOVERY FROM SUCH CONDITION AND MY DEATH IS IMMINENT, AND I AM THEREFORE UNABLE TO MAKE MY OWN HEALTHCARE DECISIONS.**

I revoke all Financial Durable Power of Attorneys that I have previously made.

This document may be revoked by me at any time, and is automatically revoked upon my death (or if I regain the ability to make my own decisions should the Power of Attorney be effective only if I become incapacitated). By placing my initials before each item below, I grant those powers of attorney to my Agent, and where there are no initials, that means that I do NOT grant those powers of attorney to my Agent. I may also cross out any powers which I do NOT wish to grant.

_____ **A. Real Estate Transactions.** The Principal authorizes the Agent to: (1) demand, receive, and obtain, by litigation or otherwise, money or other things of value to which the Principal is, may become, or claims to be entitled, and conserve, invest, disburse, or use anything so received for the purposes intended; (2) contract in any manner with any person, on terms agreeable to the Agent, to accomplish a purpose of a transaction, and perform, rescind, reform, release, or modify the contract or another contract made by or on behalf of the Principal; (3) execute, acknowledge, seal, and deliver a deed, revocation, mortgage, security agreement, lease, notice, check, promissory note, electronic funds transfer, release, or other instrument or communication the Agent considers appropriate to accomplish a purpose of a transaction; (4) prosecute, defend, submit to arbitration or mediation, settle, or propose or accept a compromise with respect to an existing claim in favor of or against the Principal or intervene in litigation relating to the claim; (5) seek on the Principal's behalf the assistance of a court to carry out an act authorized by the Principal in this Power of Attorney; (6) engage, compensate, and discharge an attorney, accountant, expert witness, or other assistant; (7) keep appropriate records of each transaction, including an accounting of receipts and disbursements; (8) prepare, execute, and file a record, report, or other document the Agent considers desirable to safeguard or promote the Principal's interest under a statute or governmental regulation; (9) reimburse the Agent for expenditures properly made by the Agent in exercising the powers granted by this Power of Attorney; and (10) in general, do any other lawful act with respect to the power and all property related to the power.

_____ **B. Tangible Personal Property.** The Principal authorizes the Agent to: (1) accept as a gift or as security for an extension of credit, reject, demand, buy, receive, or otherwise acquire ownership or possession of tangible, personal property or an interest in tangible, personal property; (2) sell, exchange, convey, with or without covenants, release, surrender, create a security interest in, grant options concerning, lease, sublease to others, or otherwise dispose of tangible, personal property or an interest in tangible, personal property; (3) release, assign, satisfy, or enforce by litigation or otherwise, a security interest, lien, or other claim on behalf of the Principal, with respect to tangible, personal property or an interest in tangible, personal property; (4) manage or conserve tangible, personal property or an interest in tangible, personal property on behalf of the Principal, including: (a) insuring against casualty, liability, or loss; (b) obtaining or regaining possession, or protecting the property or interest, by litigation or otherwise; (c) paying, compromising, or contesting taxes or assessments or applying for and receiving refunds in connection with taxes or assessments; (d) moving from place to place; (e) storing for hire or on a gratuitous bailment; and (f) using, altering, and making repairs or alterations; and (5) change the form of title of an interest in tangible, personal property.

_____ **C. Stocks and Bonds.** The Principal authorizes the Agent to: (1) buy, sell, and exchange stocks, bonds, mutual funds, and all other types of securities and financial instruments, whether held directly or indirectly, except commodity futures contracts and call and put options on stocks and stock indexes, (2) receive certificates and other evidences of ownership with respect to securities, (3) exercise voting rights with respect to securities in person or by proxy, enter into voting trusts, and consent to limitations on the right to vote.

_____ **D. Commodity and Options Transactions.** The Principal authorizes the Agent to: (1) buy, sell, exchange, assign, settle, and exercise commodity futures contracts and call and put options on stocks and stock indexes traded on a regulated option exchange, and (2) establish, continue, modify, and terminate option accounts with a broker.

_____ **E. Banking (and Other Related Financial Institutions) Transactions.** The Principal authorizes the Agent to: (1) continue, modify, and terminate an account or other banking arrangement made by, or on behalf of, the Principal; (2) establish, modify, and terminate an account or other banking arrangement with a bank, trust company, savings and loan association, credit union, thrift company, brokerage firm, or other financial institution selected by the Agent; (3) rent a safe deposit box or space in a vault; (4) contract for other services available from a financial institution as the Agent considers desirable; (5) withdraw by check, order, or otherwise money or property of the Principal deposited with, or left in, the custody of a financial institution; 6) receive bank statements, vouchers, notices, and similar documents from a financial institution and act with respect to them; (7) enter a safe deposit box or vault and withdraw or add to the contents; (8) borrow money at an interest rate agreeable to the Agent and pledge personal property of the Principal as security, when necessary, in order to borrow, pay, renew, or extend the time of payment of a debt of the Principal; (9) make, assign, draw, endorse, discount, guarantee, and negotiate promissory notes, checks, drafts, and other negotiable or nonnegotiable paper of the Principal, or payable to the Principal or the Principal's order, transfer money, receive the cash or other proceeds of those transactions, accept a draft drawn by a person upon the

Principal, and pay it when due; (10) receive for the Principal and act upon a sight draft, warehouse receipt, or other negotiable or nonnegotiable instrument; (11) apply for, receive, and use letters of credit, credit and debit cards, and traveler's checks from a financial institution and give an indemnity or other agreement in connection with letters of credit; and (12) consent to an extension of the time of payment with respect to commercial paper or a financial transaction with a financial institution.

F. Business Operating Transactions. The Principal authorizes the Agent to: (1) operate, buy, sell, enlarge, reduce, and terminate business interests; (2) act for a Principal, subject to the terms of a partnership agreement or operating agreement, to: (a) perform a duty or discharge a liability and exercise a right, power, privilege, or option that the Principal has, may have, or claims to have, under the partnership agreement or operating agreement, whether or not the Principal is a partner in a partnership or member of a limited liability company; (b) enforce the terms of any partnership agreement or operating agreement by litigation or otherwise; and (c) defend, submit to arbitration, settle, or compromise litigation to which the Principal is a party because of membership in a partnership or limited liability company; (3) exercise in person or by proxy, or enforce by litigation or otherwise, a right, power, privilege, or option the Principal has or claims to have as the holder of a bond, share, or other instrument of similar character and defend, submit to arbitration or mediation, settle, or compromise litigation to which the Principal is a party because of a bond, share, or similar instrument; (4) with respect to a business controlled by the Principal: (a) continue, modify, renegotiate, extend, and terminate a contract made by or on behalf of the Principal with respect to the business before execution of the Power of Attorney; (b) determine: (i) the location of its operation; (ii) the nature and extent of its business; (iii) the methods of manufacturing, selling, merchandising, financing, accounting, and advertising employed in its operation; (iv) the amount and types of insurance carried; and (v) the mode of engaging, compensating, and dealing with its accountants, attorneys, other Agents, and employees; (c) change the name or form of organization under which the business is operated and enter into a partnership agreement or operating agreement with other persons or organize a corporation or other business entity to take over all or part of the operation of the business; and (d) demand and receive money due or claimed by the Principal or on the Principal's behalf in the operation of the business, and control and disburse the money in the operation of the business; (5) put additional capital into a business in which the Principal has an interest; (6) join in a plan of reorganization, consolidation, or merger of the business; (7) sell or liquidate a business or part of it at the time and upon the terms the Agent considers desirable; (8) establish the value of a business under a buy-out agreement to which the Principal is a party;

(9) prepare, sign, file, and deliver reports, compilations of information, returns, or other papers with respect to a business which are required by a governmental agency or instrumentality or which the Agent considers desirable, and make related payments; and (10) pay, compromise, or contest taxes or assessments and perform any other act that the Agent considers desirable to protect the Principal from illegal or unnecessary taxation, fines, penalties, or assessments with respect to a business, including attempts to recover, in any manner permitted by law, money paid before or after the execution of this Power of Attorney.

G. Insurance and Annuities. The Principal authorizes the Agent to: (1) continue, pay the premium or assessment on, modify, rescind, release, or terminate a contract procured by or on behalf of the Principal which insures or provides an annuity to either the Principal or another person, whether or not the Principal is a beneficiary under the contract; (2) procure new, different, and additional contracts of insurance and annuities for the Principal and the Principal's spouse, children, and other dependents, and select the amount, type of insurance or annuity, and mode of payment; (3) pay the premium or assessment on, modify, rescind, release, or terminate a contract of insurance or annuity procured by the Agent; (4) apply for and receive a loan on the security of a contract of insurance or annuity; (5) surrender and receive the cash surrender value; (6) exercise an election; (7) change the manner of paying premiums; (8) change or convert the type of insurance or annuity, with respect to which the Principal has or claims to have a power described in this section; (9) apply for and procure government aid to guarantee or pay premiums of a contract of insurance on the life of the Principal; (10) collect, sell, assign, hypothecate, borrow upon, or pledge the interest of the Principal in a contract of insurance or annuity; and (11) pay from proceeds or otherwise, compromise or contest, and apply for refunds in connection with, a tax or assessment levied by a taxing authority with respect to a contract of insurance or annuity or its proceeds or liability accruing by reason of the tax or assessment.

H. Estate Transactions (Including Trusts and Other Transactions Where Principal is Beneficiary). The Principal authorizes the Agent to act for the Principal in all matters that affect a trust, probate estate, guardianship, conservatorship, escrow, custodianship, or other fund from which the Principal is, may become, or claims to be entitled, as a beneficiary, to a share or payment, including to: (1) accept, reject, disclaim, receive, receipt for, sell, assign, release, pledge, exchange, or consent to a reduction in or modification of a share in or payment from the fund; (2) demand or obtain by litigation or otherwise money or other thing of value to which the Principal is, may become, or claims to be entitled by reason of the fund; (3) initiate, participate in, and oppose litigation to ascertain the meaning, validity, or effect of a deed, will, declaration of trust, or other instrument or transaction affecting the interest of the Principal; (4) initiate, participate in, and oppose litigation to remove, substitute, or surcharge a fiduciary; (5) conserve, invest, disburse, and use anything received for an authorized purpose; and (6) transfer an interest of the Principal in real property, stocks, bonds, accounts with financial institutions or securities intermediaries, insurance, annuities, and other property, to the trustee of a revocable trust created by the Principal as settlor.

_____   **I. Claims and Litigation.** The Principal authorizes the Agent to: (1) assert and prosecute before a court or administrative agency a claim, a claim for relief, cause of action, counterclaim, offset, or defense against an individual, organization, or government, including actions to recover property or other thing of value, to recover damages sustained by the Principal, to eliminate or modify tax liability, or to seek an injunction, specific performance, or other relief; (2) bring an action to determine adverse claims, intervene in litigation, and act as amicus curiae; (3) in connection with litigation, procure an attachment, garnishment, libel, order of arrest, or other preliminary, provisional, or intermediate relief and use an available procedure to effect or satisfy a judgment, order, or decree; (4) in connection with litigation, perform any lawful act, including acceptance of tender, offer of judgment, admission of facts, submission of a controversy on an agreed statement of facts, consent to examination before trial, and binding the Principal in litigation; (5) submit to arbitration or mediation, settle, and propose or accept a compromise with respect to a claim or litigation; (6) waive the issuance and service of process upon the Principal, accept service of process, appear for the Principal, designate persons upon whom process directed to the Principal may be served, execute and file or deliver stipulations on the Principal's behalf, verify pleadings, seek appellate review, procure and give surety and indemnity bonds, contract and pay for the preparation and printing of records and briefs, receive and execute and file or deliver a consent, waiver, release, confession of judgment, satisfaction of judgment, notice, agreement, or other instrument in connection with the prosecution, settlement, or defense of a claim or litigation; (7) act for the Principal with respect to bankruptcy or insolvency, whether voluntary or involuntary, concerning the Principal or some other person, or with respect to a reorganization, receivership, or application for the appointment of a receiver or trustee which affects an interest of the Principal in property or other thing of value; and (8) pay a judgment against the Principal or a settlement made in connection with litigation and receive and conserve money or other thing of value paid in settlement of or as proceeds of a claim or litigation.

_____   **J. Personal and Family Maintenance.** The Principal authorizes the Agent to: (1) perform the acts necessary to maintain the customary standard of living of the

Principal, the Principal's spouse, children, and other individuals customarily or legally entitled to be supported by the Principal, including providing living quarters by purchase, lease, or other contract, or paying the operating costs, including interest, amortization payments, repairs, and taxes, on premises owned by the Principal and occupied by those individuals; (2) provide for the individuals described under (1) normal domestic help, usual vacations and travel expenses, and funds for shelter, clothing, food, appropriate education, and other current living costs; (3) pay on behalf of the individuals described under (1) expenses for necessary medical, dental, and surgical care, hospitalization, and custodial care; (4) act as the Principal's personal representative pursuant to the Social Security Act, and applicable regulations, in making decisions related to the past, present, or future payment for the provision of healthcare consented to by the Principal or anyone authorized under the law of this state to consent to healthcare on behalf of the Principal; (5) continue any provision made by the Principal, for the individuals described under (1), for automobiles or other means of transportation, including registering, licensing, insuring, and replacing them; (6) maintain or open charge accounts for the convenience of the individuals described under (1) and open new accounts the Agent considers desirable to accomplish a lawful purpose; and (7) continue payments incidental to the membership or affiliation of the Principal in a church, club, society, order, or other organization or to continue contributions to those organizations.

K. Benefits From Social Security, Medicare, Medicaid, Military Service, Other Government Programs. The Principal authorizes the Agent to: (1) execute vouchers in the name of the Principal for allowances and reimbursements payable by the United States or a foreign government or by a state or subdivision of a state to the Principal, including allowances and reimbursements for transportation of the individuals, and for shipment of their household effects; (2) take possession and order the removal and shipment of property of the Principal from a post, warehouse, depot, dock, or other place of storage or safekeeping, either governmental or private, and execute and deliver a release, voucher, receipt, bill of lading, shipping ticket, certificate, or other instrument for that purpose; (3) prepare, file, and prosecute a claim of the Principal to a benefit or assistance, financial or otherwise, to which the Principal claims to be entitled under a statute or governmental regulation; (4) prosecute, defend, submit to arbitration or mediation, settle, and propose or accept a compromise with respect to any benefit or assistance the Principal may be entitled to receive under a statute or governmental regulation; and (5) receive the financial proceeds of a claims and conserve, invest, disburse, or use anything so received for a lawful purpose. I intend for my attorney-in-fact under this Power of Attorney to be treated as I would be with respect to my rights regarding the use and disclosure of my individually identifiable health information or other medical records. This release authority applies to any information governed by the Health Insurance Portability and Accountability Act of 1996 (a.k.a. HIPAA).

L. Records, Reports and Statements. The Principal authorizes the Agent to: (1) demand, receive, and obtain by litigation or otherwise acquire any record, reports, or other written statements regarding the Principal; (2) create, modify, or retain profession regarding documents needed on behalf of the Principal related to financial matters; (3) provide written responses to inquiries about Principal regarding financial matters.

M. Retirement Benefit Transactions. The Principal authorizes the Agent to: (1) select a payment option under a retirement plan in which the Principal participates, including a plan for a self-employed individual; (2) make voluntary contributions to those plans; (3) exercise the investment powers available under a self-directed retirement plan; (4) make a rollover of benefits into another retirement plan; (5) if authorized by the plan, borrow from, sell assets to, purchase assets from, or request distributions from the plan; and (6) waive the right of the Principal to be a beneficiary of a joint or survivor annuity if the Principal is a spouse who is not employed.

N. Making Gifts To My Spouse, Children, More Remote Descendants, Parents, and Others. The Principal authorizes the Agent to make gifts of any of the Principal's property to individuals or organizations within the limits of the annual exclusion under the Internal Revenue Code as the Agent determines to be in the Principal's best interest based on all relevant factors, including:(1) the value and nature of the Principal's property; (2) the Principal's foreseeable obligations and need for maintenance; 3) minimization of income, estate, inheritance, generation-skipping transfer or gift taxes; (4) eligibility for public benefits or assistance under a statute or governmental regulation; and (5) the Principal's personal history of making or joining in making gifts.

O. Tax Matters. The Principal authorizes the Agent to: (1) prepare, sign, and file Federal, state, local, and foreign income, gift, payroll, Federal Insurance Contributions Act, and other tax returns, claims for refunds, requests for extension of time, petitions regarding tax matters, and any other tax-related documents, including receipts, offers, waivers, consents, including consents and agreements under the Internal Revenue Code, closing agreements, and any Power of Attorney required by the Internal Revenue Service or other taxing authority with respect to a tax year upon which the statute of limitations has not run; (2) pay taxes due, collect refunds, post bonds, receive confidential information, and contest deficiencies determined by the Internal Revenue Service or other taxing authority;

(3) exercise any election available to the Principal under Federal, state, local, or foreign tax law; and (4) act for the Principal in all tax matters for all periods before the Internal Revenue Service, and any other taxing authority.

P. Other Matters. _____

_____

_____

_____

_____

_____

_____

_____

Q. All Other Financial Matters. Those matters not mentioned in this document are to be covered by this provision.

R. Full and Unqualified Authority to My Agent to Delegate Any or All of the Foregoing Powers To Any Person or Persons Whom My Agent May Select.

S. Unlimited Power and Authority To Act In All Of The Above Situations (A Through R) Which I Have Initialed. The Principal authorizes the Agent to: (1) demand, receive, and obtain by litigation or otherwise, money or other thing of value to which the Principal is, may become, or claims to be entitled, and conserve, invest, disburse, or use anything so received for the purposes intended; (2) contract in any manner with any person, on terms agreeable to the Agent, to accomplish a purpose of a transaction, and perform, rescind, reform, release, or modify the contract or another contract made by or on behalf of the Principal; (3) execute, acknowledge, seal, and deliver a deed, revocation, mortgage, security agreement, lease, notice, check, promissory note, electronic funds transfer, release, or other instrument or communication the Agent considers desirable to accomplish a purpose of a transaction, including creating a schedule of the Principal's property and attaching it to the Power of Attorney; (4) prosecute, defend, submit to arbitration or mediation, settle, and propose or accept a compromise with respect to, a claim existing in favor of or against the Principal or intervene in litigation relating to the claim; (5) seek on the Principal's behalf the assistance of a court to carry out an act authorized by the Principal in the Power of

Attorney; (6) engage, compensate, and discharge an attorney, accountant, expert witness, or other assistant; (7) keep appropriate records of each transaction, including an accounting of receipts and disbursements; (8) prepare, execute, and file a record, report, or other document the Agent considers desirable to safeguard or promote the Principal's interest under a statute or governmental regulation; (9) reimburse the Agent for expenditures properly made by the Agent in exercising the powers granted by the Power of Attorney; and (10) in general, do any other lawful act with respect to the power and all property related to the power.

I specifically DO NOT want the following person(s) to be involved in any manner in the decision-making regarding my financial matters: _____

_____.

To induce any third party to rely upon this Power of Attorney, I agree that any third party receiving a signed copy or facsimile of this document may rely upon such copy, and that revocation or termination of this Power of Attorney is ineffective as to such third party until actual notice or knowledge of such revocation or termination has been received by the third party.

My attorney-in-fact receives NO compensation for providing this service, or be liable to me, my estate, heirs, successors, or assigns for acting or refraining from acting under this document, except for willful misconduct or gross negligence.

I, _____, the Principal, sign my name to this

Power of Attorney this _____day of _____and, being first duly sworn, do declare to the undersigned authority that I sign and execute this instrument as my Power of Attorney and that I sign it willingly, or willingly direct another to sign for me, that I execute it as my free and voluntary act for the purposes expressed in the Power of Attorney and that I am eighteen years of age or older, of sound mind and under no constraint or undue influence, and that I have read and understand the contents of the notice at the beginning of this document.

Principal Signature: _____Date: _____

WITNESS STATEMENT

On this _____ day of _____ 20 _____ we, _____

and _____, declare under penalty of perjury that the person who signed or acknowledged this document is personally known to me (or proved to me on the basis of convincing evidence) to be the Principal, that the Principal signed or acknowledged this durable Power of Attorney in my presence, that the Principal appears to be of sound mind and under no duress, fraud, or undue influence. We are not appointed as an Agent by this document. We are not related to the Principal by blood, marriage, or adoption. We would not be entitled to any portion of the Principal's estate on the Principal's death. We are not the attending physician of the Principal or an employee of the attending physician. We have no claim against any portion of the Principal's estate on the Principal's death. Furthermore, if we are an employee of a healthcare facility in which the Principal is a patient, we are not involved in providing direct patient care to the Principal and are not employed as an officer, director, partner, or business office employee of the healthcare facility or of any parent organization of the healthcare facility.

I sign my name to the foregoing Power of Attorney being first duly sworn and do declare to the undersigned authority that the Principal signs and executes this instrument as his/her Power of Attorney and that he\she signs it willingly, or willingly directs another to sign for him/her, and that I, in the presence and hearing of the Principal, sign this Power of Attorney as witness to the Principal's signing and that to the best of my knowledge the Principal is eighteen years of age or older, is of sound mind, and is under no constraint or undue influence.

_____   _____
Witness's Signature   Printed Name of Witness

_____
Address of Witness

_____   _____
Witness's Signature   Printed Name of Witness

_____
Address of Witness

_____   _____
Witness's Signature   Printed Name of Witness

_____
Address of Witness

NOTARY PUBLIC ACKNOWLEDGEMENT

The foregoing instrument was acknowledged, subscribed, and sworn to before me, this _____day of _____, 20____, by _____, and witnessed by _____, and _____, personally known to me (or proved to me on the basis of satisfactory evidence) to be the person whose name is subscribed to the foregoing instrument, and acknowledged to me that he or she executed the same in his or her authorized capacity and that by his or her signature on the instrument, the person, or the entity upon behalf of which the person acted, executed the instrument.

Witness my hand and official seal.

_____

NOTARY PUBLIC for the State of _____

My Commission Expires: _____

[For Notary Seal or Stamp]

_____
NOTARY PUBLIC

POWER OF ATTORNEY ACKNOWLEDGEMENT AND ACCEPTANCE BY AGENT AND ALTERNATE AGENT

I, _____, have read the attached Power of Attorney, and I am the person identified as the Agent with the Financial Durable Power of Attorney for the Principal. I hereby acknowledge that I accept my appointment as Agent and attorney-in-fact, and, when I act as Agent, I will exercise the powers for the benefit of the Principal. I will keep the assets of the Principal separate from my assets, personal, professional, or otherwise. I will exercise reasonable caution and prudence, and I will keep a full and accurate record of all actions, receipts, and disbursements on behalf of the Principal.

Agent Signature: _____Date: _____

I, _____, have read the attached Power of Attorney, and I agree to act as an alternative Agent if the person identified as the Agent with the Financial Durable Power of Attorney for the Principal does not or cannot accept these duties. I accept my appointment as alternate Agent and attorney-in-fact, and if I am called upon to act as Agent, I will exercise the powers for the benefit of the Principal. I will keep the assets of the Principal separate from my assets, personal, professional, or otherwise. I will exercise reasonable caution and prudence, and I will keep a full and accurate record of all actions, receipts, and disbursements on behalf of the Principal.

Alternated Agent Signature: _____Date: _____

Power of Attorney

Cover Page

**Power of Attorney
New York Statutory Major Gifts Rider**

Of

_____

Date Created: _____

Notes:

Source: N.Y. Gen. Oblig. Law § 5-1514(10).

POWER OF ATTORNEY
NEW YORK STATUTORY MAJOR GIFTS RIDER
AUTHORIZATION TO MAKE MAJOR GIFTS OR OTHER TRANSFERS

CAUTION TO THE PRINCIPAL: This OPTIONAL rider allows you to authorize your agent to make major gifts or other transfers of your money or other property during your lifetime. Granting any of the following authority to your agent gives your agent the authority to take actions which could significantly reduce your property or change how your property is distributed at your death. "Major gifts or other transfers" are described in section 5-1514 of the General Obligations Law. This Major Gifts Rider does not require your agent to exercise granted authority, but when he or she exercises this authority, he or she must act according to any instructions you provide, or otherwise in your best interest.

This Major Gifts Rider and the Power of Attorney it supplements must be read together as a single instrument.

Before signing this document authorizing your agent to make major gifts and other transfers, you should seek legal advice to ensure that your intentions are clearly and properly expressed.

(a) GRANT OF LIMITED AUTHORITY TO MAKE GIFTS

Granting gifting authority to your agent gives your agent the authority to take actions which could significantly reduce your property.

If you wish to allow your agent to make gifts to himself or herself, you must separately grant that authority in subdivision (c) below.

To grant your agent the gifting authority provided below, initial the bracket to the left of the authority.

[Initial here](   ) I grant authority to my agent to make gifts to my spouse, children and more remote descendants, and parents, not to exceed, for each donee, the annual federal gift tax exclusion amount pursuant to the Internal Revenue Code. For gifts to my children and more remote descendants, and parents, the maximum amount of the gift to each donee shall not exceed twice the gift tax exclusion amount, if my spouse agrees to split gift treatment pursuant to the Internal Revenue Code. This authority must be exercised pursuant to my instructions, or otherwise for purposes which the agent reasonably deems to be in my best interest.

(b) MODIFICATIONS:

Use this section if you wish to authorize gifts in excess of the above amount, gifts to other beneficiaries or other types of transfers. Granting such authority to your agent gives your agent the authority to take actions which could significantly reduce your property and/or change how your property is distributed at your death. If you wish to authorize your agent to make gifts or transfers to himself or herself, you must separately grant that authority in subdivision (c) below.

Source: N.Y. Gen. Oblig. Law § 5-1514(10).

[Initial here](   ) I grant the following authority to my agent to make gifts or transfers pursuant to my instructions, or otherwise for purposes which the agent reasonably deems to be in my best interest:

(c) GRANT OF SPECIFIC AUTHORITY FOR AN AGENT TO MAKE MAJOR GIFTS OR OTHER TRANSFERS TO HIMSELF OR HERSELF: (OPTIONAL)

If you wish to authorize your agent to make gifts or transfers to himself or herself, you must grant that authority in this section, indicating to which agent(s) the authorization is granted, and any limitations and guidelines.

[Initial here](   ) I grant specific authority for the following agent(s) to make the following major gifts or other transfers to himself or herself:

This authority must be exercised pursuant to my instructions, or otherwise for purposes which the agent reasonably deems to be in my best interest.

(d) ACCEPTANCE BY THIRD PARTIES:

I agree to indemnify the third party for any claims that may arise against the third party because of reliance on this Major Gifts Rider.

(e) SIGNATURE OF PRINCIPAL AND ACKNOWLEDGMENT:

In Witness Whereof I have hereunto signed my name on _____, 20____.

PRINCIPAL signs here: _____ (acknowledgement)

Source: N.Y. Gen. Oblig. Law § 5-1514(10).

(f) SIGNATURES OF WITNESSES:

By signing as a witness, I acknowledge that the principal signed the Major Gifts Rider in my presence and the presence of the other witness, or that the principal acknowledged to me that the principal's signature was affixed by him or her or at his or her direction. I also acknowledge that the principal has stated that this Major Gifts Rider reflects his or her wishes and that he or she has signed it voluntarily. I am not named herein as a permissible recipient of major gifts.

_____	_____
Signature of witness 1	Signature of witness 2
_____	_____
Date	Date
_____	_____
Print name	Print name
_____	_____
Address	Address
_____	_____
City, State, Zip code	City, State, Zip code

(g) This document prepared by: _____

Power of Attorney

Cover Page

Minor Child Care Limited Power of Attorney

Of

_____

Date Created: _____

Notes:

MINOR CHILD CARE LIMITED POWER OF ATTORNEY

I/We, _____,

whose address is _____

City of _____, in the County of _____,

in the State of _____, are the legal guardian(s) ("GUARDIAN") of the
following minor child(ren):

Name: _____DOB: _____

Name: _____DOB: _____

Name: _____DOB: _____

(Collectively referred to as "CHILD") grant a limited and specific power of attorney to, and do

hereby appoint _____, whose address is

_____City _____,

County_____, State _____, "AGENT,"

and if Agent is unable or unwilling to make those decisions, I appoint as an alternate Agent

_____, whose address is _____

_____County_____

City_____in the State of _____.

Agent will act as attorney-in-fact and to have the full power and authority to perform only the
following acts that are **initialed below,** on Guardian's behalf, to the same extent Guardian could
do so personally if Guardian were personally present, with respect to the following matter to the
extent that Guardian is permitted by law to act through an agent. Consent given to:

_____   any necessary medical treatment for the Child, including any emergency medical
treatment, surgery, medication, hospitalization, any x-ray examination, anesthetic,
medical or surgical diagnosis or treatment, and hospital care which is deemed
advisable by, and is to be rendered under the general or specific supervision of
any physician and surgeon licensed under the provision of the Medical Practice
Act, whether such diagnosis or treatment is rendered at the office of said
physician or at a hospital, or any other necessary medical treatment; that may be

required. It is understood that this power is given in advance of any specific diagnosis, treatment, or hospital care being required, but is given to provide authority and power on the part of our Agent to give specific consent to any and all such diagnosis, treatment, or hospital care which the aforementioned physician in the exercise of his or her best judgment may deem advisable;

_____ enroll and withdraw the Child from any school or child care facility, and it is expressly the intent of Guardian that the Agent is given wide discretion in education matters and that all educational institutions recognize and follow the instructions of the Agent in regards to the education of the Child;

_____ exercise the same parental rights that Guardian may personally exercise regarding the care, custody and control of the Child, including providing discipline;

_____ authorize Agent to execute, acknowledge and deliver any instrument under seal or otherwise, and to do all things necessary to carry out the intent granted to Agent and authorize Agent to act fully and effectually as the Guardians may do if personally present, limited, however, to the purpose for which this limited power of attorney is executed.

_____ allow Agent to continue with the powers of attorney granted in this document even if any Guardian may become incapacitated or disabled, and Agent will only loose powers if Guardian revokes those powers which Guardian can do at any time either written or oral.

To induce any third party to rely on this Power of Attorney, any third party receiving a signed copy or facsimile of this document may rely on such copy, and that revocation or termination of this Power of Attorney is ineffective as to such third party until actual notice or knowledge of such revocation or termination has been received by the third party.

Agent receives NO compensation for providing this service, or will be liable to me, my estate, heirs, successors, or assigns for acting or refraining from acting under this document, except for willful misconduct or gross negligence.

I/We, _____,

the Guardian, sign to this Power of Attorney this _____ day of _____,

20_____ and, being first duly sworn, do declare to the undersigned authority sign and execute this instrument and sign willingly, or willingly direct another to sign for me, execute this Power of Attorney as a free and voluntary act for the purposes expressed in the Power of Attorney and am eighteen years of age or older, of sound mind and under no constraint or undue influence, and have read and understand the contents of the notice at the beginning of this document.

Guardian(s) Signature(s): _____

_____

Date: _____

WITNESS STATEMENT

On this _____ day of _____, 20_____, we, _____

and _____, declare under penalty of perjury that the person(s) who signed or acknowledged this document is personally known to me (or proved to me on the basis of convincing evidence) to be the Guardian, that the Guardian signed or acknowledged this durable Power of Attorney in my presence, that the Guardian appears to be of sound mind and under no duress, fraud, or undue influence. We are not appointed as an Agent by this document. We are not related to the Guardian by blood, marriage, or adoption.

I sign my name to the foregoing Power of Attorney being first duly sworn and do declare to the undersigned authority that the Guardian signs and executes this instrument as his/her Power of Attorney and that he\she signs it willingly, or willingly directs another to sign for him/her, and that I, in the presence and hearing of the Guardian, sign this Power of Attorney as witness to the Guardian's signing and that to the best of my knowledge the Guardian is eighteen years of age or older, of sound mind and under no constraint or undue influence.

_____   _____
Witness's Signature   Printed Name of Witness

_____
Address of Witness

_____   _____
Witness's Signature   Printed Name of Witness

_____
Address of Witness

NOTARY PUBLIC ACKNOWLEDGEMENT

The foregoing instrument was acknowledged, subscribed, and sworn to before me, this _____ day

of _____, 20____, by _____, and witnessed

by _____, and _____,
personally known to me (or proved to me on the basis of satisfactory evidence) to be the person
whose name is subscribed to the foregoing instrument, and acknowledged to me that he or she
executed the same in his or her authorized capacity and that by his or her signature on the
instrument, the person, or the entity upon behalf of which the person acted, executed the
instrument.

Witness my hand and official seal.

_____

NOTARY PUBLIC for the State of _____

My Commission Expires: _____

[For Notary Seal or Stamp]

_____
NOTARY PUBLIC

MINOR CHILD CARE LIMITED POWER OF ATTORNEY ACKNOWLEDGEMENT AND ACCEPTANCE BY AGENT AND ALTERNATE AGENT

I, _____, have read the attached Power of Attorney, and I am the person identified as the Agent with the Minor Child Care Limited Power of Attorney. I hereby acknowledge that I accept my appointment as Agent and attorney-in-fact, and when I act as Agent I will exercise the powers for the benefit of the Guardian. I will exercise reasonable caution and prudence, and I will keep a full and accurate record of all actions, receipts, and disbursements on behalf of the Guardian.

Agent Signature: _____Date: _____

I, _____, have read the attached Power of Attorney, and I agree to act as an alternative Agent if the person identified as the Agent with the Minor Child Care Limited Power of Attorney does not or cannot accept these duties. I accept my appointment as alternate Agent and attorney-in-fact, and if I am called on to act as Agent I will exercise the powers for the benefit of the Guardian and Child. I will exercise reasonable caution and prudence, and I will keep a full and accurate record of all actions, receipts, and disbursements on behalf of the Guardian.

Alternated Agent Signature: _____ Date: _____

Power of Attorney

Cover Page

Power of Attorney Revocation

Of

_____

Date Created: _____

Notes:

POWER OF ATTORNEY REVOCATION

I/We, _____,

whose address is _____

City_____, County_____,

State_____, revoke the Power of Attorney dated_____

with the title _____and appointed Agent

_____whose address is_____

_____City _____,

County _____, State _____, and alternate Agent

_____, whose address is_____

_____, City_____,

County_____, State_____, in its entirety
without limitations, including revoking any appointment of any persons named in the above
Power of Attorney, the Agent, and the alternate Agent named in the document.

Revoking party's signature: _____Date: _____

NOTARY PUBLIC ACKNOWLEDGEMENT

The foregoing instrument was acknowledged, subscribed, and sworn to before me,

_____this _____day of _____,

20_____, personally known to me (or proved to me on the basis of satisfactory evidence) to be the
person whose name is subscribed to the foregoing instrument, and acknowledged to me that he or
she executed the same in his or her authorized capacity and that by his or her signature on the
instrument, the person, or the entity upon behalf of which the person acted, executed the
instrument.
Witness my hand and official seal.
NOTARY PUBLIC for the State of _____, County of _____

My Commission Expires: _____

[For Notary Seal or Stamp]

_____
NOTARY PUBLIC

Trusts

Trusts Checklist

❏ If you are in the State of Florida or Florida is the State where this Living Trust will be legal, then you must also complete the Florida Witness Statement for Living Trusts (included in this book). No other State requires a witness to a Living Trust.

❏ Make additional copies of any specific pages you may need or tear them out of the book.

❏ Read over the blank form.

❏ If there are parts of the form you do not understand, read the applicable section within this book.

❏ Make adjustments to the form to meet your needs. If the paragraph or portion of the sample form does not apply, write "Does not apply" in the blank space.

❏ Complete the portions of the sample form with blank spaces. (Do NOT sign just yet.)

❏ Review the Living Trust you have completed to ensure that you have completed the entire form.

❏ Review the State Specific Information at PeerlessLegal.com.

❏ Meet with a Notary Public.

❏ Double-check the Living Trust for completeness and you understand its contents.

❏ Sign and date the Living Trust in the presence of the Notary Public.

❏ If your Living Trust is complicated, or includes numerous additions, then do not use this book or its contents for the sole purpose of creating a Living Trust. Contact a licensed attorney to help you create a Living Trust that meets your specific needs.

❏ Give a copy of the Living Trust to the named Successor Trustee and to the alternative Successor Trustee.

❏ Store a record of your final, signed Living Trust, in a safe place, along with all of your other important documents that you wish to pass on.

Trusts

Cover Page

Living Trust (Single Person)

Of

_____

Date Created: _____

Notes:

DECLARATION OF TRUST (Single Person)—LIVING TRUST
OF _____

This DECLARATION OF TRUST ("DECLARATION") creates a trust known as The _____
_____Living Trust, and is entered into on this date
_____("TRUST").

1. **ESTABLISHMENT OF TRUST.** This Declaration creates a Trust between _____
_____("GRANTOR"), and himself/herself as
"TRUSTEE," whose address is _____
_____City _____,
County _____, State _____.

   A. **CHOICE OF LAW.** The Trust will be governed by the laws of the State of
   _____, and all Trusts created by this Declaration, including
   Child's Trust, and actions taken by Trustee, are governed under this State's laws,
   subject to the Trustee's fiduciary duty to the Grantor and beneficiaries.

   B. **SEVERABILITY.** If any provision of this Declaration of Trust is ruled
   unenforceable, the remaining provisions will remain in effect.

   C. **AMENDMENTS.** This Trust includes any provisions added by amendments.

2. **TRUST PROPERTY.** Grantor has transferred, or will transfer, to the Trustee, the
   property that may be added to this Declaration in "**Schedule A**—Property Placed in
   Trust," including after-acquired property, that will be used for the benefit of the trust
   beneficiaries, and will be administered and distributed by the Trustee in accordance with
   this Declaration. Grantor is the legal and beneficial owner of all property in this
   Declaration and all property that may be added.

3. **POWERS OF THE GRANTOR.** The Grantor has the powers deemed necessary and
   appropriate to administer this Trust, including powers granted by the State where this
   Declaration is governed and is subject to the fiduciary duties to the Grantor and
   beneficiaries. The powers of this Declaration include, but are not limited to, the powers
   to:

A. AMEND OR REVOKE DECLARATION.

1)   **BY GRANTOR.** The Grantor reserves the power to amend or revoke this Declaration at any time during Grantor's lifetime, without notifying any beneficiary.

2)   **BY OTHERS.** The right to amend or revoke this Declaration is personal to the Grantor, and any conservator, guardian, or other party may NOT exercise Grantor's power to amend or revoke this Declaration without the Grantor specifically granting the power in a separate Durable Power of Attorney.

B. RETAIN ALL RIGHTS TO TRUST PROPERTY. All rights to any income, profits, and control of the Trust property are retained by the Grantor until the death of the Grantor.

C. HOMESTEAD. If the Grantor's principal residence is held in this Trust, Grantor has the right to possess and occupy the residence for Grantor's entire life, rent-free and without charge, except for taxes, insurance, maintenance, and related costs and expenses. This right is intended to give Grantor a beneficial interest in the property and to ensure that Grantor does not lose eligibility for any State homestead tax exemption for which Grantor otherwise qualifies.

D. INCAPACITY OF GRANTOR. If Grantor becomes incapacitated, physically or mentally, to where Grantor cannot manage this Trust then, whether or not a court has declared the Grantor incompetent or in need of conservator or guardian, the person(s) named as Successor Trustee will serve as Trustee (as defined in Section 4.B.). The determination of the Grantor's capacity to manage this Trust will be made by the Successor Trustee (as defined in Section 4.B.) who is reasonably available to make such a determination in a timely manner. If there are multiple successor trustees, and a majority of the Successor Trustees (as defined in Section 4.B.) state, in writing, that, in their opinion, Grantor is no longer reasonably capable of serving as trustee, the Successor Trustee (as defined in Section 4.B.) will serve as Trustee. The Successor Trustee (as defined in Section 4.B.) will pay

trust income, at least annually, to, or for the benefit of, the Grantor and may spend any amount of Trust principal necessary for the needs of the Grantor, until the Grantor is no longer incapacitated or until the Grantor's death.

E. **DEATH OF GRANTOR.** At Grantor's death, this Trust will become irrevocable. This Trust cannot be altered or amended, except as provided in this Declaration, and it may NOT be terminated except through distributions permitted by this Declaration. Trustee must pay out Trust property necessary for payment of the Grantor's debts, estate taxes, and expenses of the Grantor's illnesses and cost of final arrangements, such as burial plot or cremation costs. All of the property in the Trust must be distributed outright to the Beneficiaries (as provided in Section 5.A.) subject to any provisions in this Declaration that creates child's trusts or creates custodianships under the Uniform Transfers to Minors Act.

4. **TRUSTEES.**

   A. **TRUSTEE.** The Trustee is identified in Section 1. Establishment of Trust.

   B. **SUCCESSOR TRUSTEE.** Upon the death or incapacity (as defined in Section 3.D. and Section 3.E.) of the Trustee, _____ will serve as the "SUCCESSOR TRUSTEE." The Successor Trustee will become the Trustee at that time. If the Successor Trustee is not able to serve or continue to serve as successor trustee, then the alternate Successor Trustee will be _____ _____.

   _____ The Successor Trustee will have the complete and independent authority to act for, and represent the Trust.

   [OR] (Select only one by placing your initials next to the clause.)

   _____ The Successor Trustee must obtain consent, in writing, from all of the beneficiaries whose Trust property is affected by a transaction.

   C. **TRUSTEE'S RESPONSIBILITY.** The Trustee will serve as Trustee of all of the Trusts created in this Declaration, including any Child's Trust.

D. TRUSTEE RESIGNATION. Any Trustee may resign at any time by signing a notice of resignation and must deliver the notice of registration to the alternate Trustee under Section 4.B.

E. POWERS AND DUTIES.

1) **POWERS TO APPOINT SUCCESSOR TRUSTEE.** If the entire successor Trustees named in this Declaration, Section 4.B. cease to, or are unable to, serve as Trustee, any Trustee may appoint an additional Trustee or Successor Trustee to serve in the order nominated. The appointment must be made in writing, signed by the Trustee, and notarized.

2) **SPECIFIC DUTIES.** The Trustee's powers include, but are not limited to, the power to:

1. sell Trust property, and borrow money and to encumber Trust property, including mortgage, deed by trust, or otherwise, any Trust real estate.

2. manage Trust real estate as if the Trustee were the absolute owner, including the power to lease (even lease terms that extend beyond the period of the Trust), grant options to lease Trust real estate, make repairs or alterations, and to insure against loss.

3. sell or grant options for the sale or exchange of any Trust property, including stocks, bonds, debentures, and any other form of security or security account, at public or private sale for cash or credit.

4. invest Trust property in property of any kind, including, but not limited to, bonds, debentures, notes, mortgages, stocks, stock options, stock futures, and buying on margin.

5. receive additional property from any source and add to any Trust created by this Declaration.

6. employ and pay reasonable fees to accountants, lawyers, or

investment experts for information or advice relating to the Trust.

7. deposit and hold Trust funds in both interest-bearing and non-interest-bearing accounts.

8. deposit funds in bank or other accounts insured or uninsured by the FDIC.

9. enter into electronic fund transfer or safe deposit arrangements with financial institutions.

10. continue any business of the Grantor.

11. institute or defend legal actions concerning the Trust or Grantor's affairs.

12. execute any document necessary to administer any Child's Trust created in this Declaration.

13. diversify investments, including authority to decide that some or all of the Trust property need not produce income.

3) **PAYMENT OF DEBTS AND TA.** The Grantor's debts and death taxes are to be paid by the Trustee from the following Trust property: _____

_____.

If the property is not sufficient to pay all the Grantor's debts and death taxes, then the Trustee must make a determination as to how such debts and death taxes will be paid from Trust property.

4) **ACCOUNTING.** No accountings or similar reports are required by Trustee.

F. **NO TRUSTEE BOND REQUIRED.** No bond is required of any Trustee.

G. **NO TRUSTEE COMPENSATION.** No Trustee is to receive any compensation in any form for serving as Trustee, except that a Trustee may be entitled to reasonable compensation, as determined by the Trustee, for serving as a Trustee of a Child's Trust created by this Declaration, or for serving as Trustee if the Grantor is incapacitated.

H. TRUSTEE LIABILITY. With respect to the exercise or non-exercise of discretionary powers granted by this Declaration, the Trustee is not liable for actions taken in good faith.

5. **BENEFICIARIES.** On Grantor's death, the property listed on **Schedule A** is to be distributed to the beneficiaries named in this Section.

    A. PRIMARY AND ALTERNATE BENEFICIARIES.

        1)   The property identified as _____

_____

_____

is left in Trust to _____

(the "PRIMARY BENEFICIARY"). If the primary beneficiary does not survive Grantor, or rejects the property, then to _____

_____

(the "ALTERNATE PRIMARY BENEFICIARY").

        2)   The property identified as _____

_____

_____

is left in Trust to _____

(the "PRIMARY BENEFICIARY"). If the primary beneficiary does not survive Grantor, or rejects the property, then to _____

_____

(the "ALTERNATE PRIMARY BENEFICIARY").

        3)   The property identified as _____

_____

_____

is left in Trust to _____

(the "PRIMARY BENEFICIARY"). If the primary beneficiary does not survive Grantor, or rejects the property, then to _____

_____

(the "ALTERNATE PRIMARY BENEFICIARY").

B. RESIDUARY BENEFICIARY. The remainder of the property in **Schedule A** that is not assigned and validly disposed of in Section 5.A. or 6.F. will go to _____

_____

("RESIDUARY BENEFICIARY") and if the Residuary Beneficiary does not take the property then _____

will take the property as the "ALTERNATE RESIDUARY BENEFICIARY."

6. **CHILD(REN)'S SUBTRUST(S).** All Trust property left to any of the minor or young adult beneficiaries listed below in Section 6.A. will be retained in Trust for each named child beneficiary in a separate Trust that can be identified and referred to by adding the name of that Trust's beneficiary to the name of this Trust. The following terms apply to each Child's Trust:

   A. TRUST BENEFICIARIES AND AGE LIMITS. A Child's Trust ends when the beneficiary of that Trust becomes 35, except as otherwise specified in this Section:

   Trust for   Ends at Age

   _____   _____

   _____   _____

   _____   _____

   _____   _____

   _____   _____

   B. TRUSTEE POWERS AND DUTIES.

   1)   Until a Child's Trust ends, the Trustee may distribute or use assets for the benefit of the beneficiary as the Trustee deems necessary for the beneficiary's health, support, maintenance, or education. Education includes, but is not limited to, college, graduate, professional, and vocational studies, and reasonably related living expenses.

2)   In deciding whether to make a distribution to the beneficiary, the Trustee may take into account the beneficiary's other income, resources, and sources of support.

3)   Any Child's Trust income that is not distributed to a beneficiary by the Trustee will accumulate and add to the principal of the Trust for that beneficiary.

4)   The Trustee of a Child's Trust is not required to make any accounting or report to the Trust beneficiary.

C. NO ASSIGNMENT OF BENEFICIARY INTEREST. The interests of the beneficiary of a Child's Trust cannot be transferred by voluntary or involuntary assignment or by operation of law before actual receipt by the beneficiary. These interests are free from the claims of creditors and from attachments, execution, bankruptcy, or other legal process to the fullest extent permitted by law.

D. TRUSTEE COMPENSATION. Any Trustee of a Child's Trust created under this Declaration will be entitled to reasonable compensation out of the Trust assets for ordinary and extraordinary services, and for all services in connection with the termination of any Trust.

E. TERMINATION. A Child's Trust will end when any of the following events occur:

1)   the beneficiary reaches the age specified in Section 6.A. If the Trust ends for this reason, the remaining principal and accumulated income of the Trust will be given outright to the beneficiary.

2)   the beneficiary dies. If the Trust ends for this reason, the Trust property will pass to the beneficiary's heirs.

3)   the Trustee distributes all Trust property under the provisions of this Declaration.

F. CUSTODIANSHIPS UNDER THE UNIFORM TRANSFERS TO MINORS ACT.

1) All property that the minor beneficiary, _____, is entitled to under this Trust is given to _____ to act as custodian for the beneficiary under the State of _____ Uniform Transfers to Minors Act, until the beneficiary reaches the age _____.

2) All property that the minor beneficiary, _____, is entitled to under this Trust is given to _____ to act as custodian for the beneficiary under the State of _____ Uniform Transfers to Minors Act, until the beneficiary reaches the age _____.

3) All property that the minor beneficiary, _____, is entitled to under this Trust is given to _____ to act as custodian for the beneficiary under the State of _____ Uniform Transfers to Minors Act, until the beneficiary reaches the age _____.

4) All property that the minor beneficiary, _____, is entitled to under this Trust is given to _____ to act as custodian for the beneficiary under the State of _____ Uniform Transfers to Minors Act, until the beneficiary reaches the age _____.

CERTIFICATION BY GRANTOR. I certify that I have read this Declaration and that it correctly states the terms and conditions under which the Trust property is to be held, managed, and disposed of by the Trustee, and I approve the Declaration.

_____   _____

Grantor and Trustee   Date

NOTARY PUBLIC ACKNOWLEDGEMENT

The foregoing instrument was acknowledged, subscribed, and sworn to before me,

_____ this ____day of ___, 20_____, personally known to me (or proved to me on the basis of satisfactory evidence) to be the person whose name is subscribed to the foregoing instrument, and acknowledged to me that he or she executed the same in his or her authorized capacity and that by his or her signature on the instrument, the person, or the entity upon behalf of which the person acted, executed the instrument.

Witness my hand and official seal.

_____

NOTARY PUBLIC for the State of _____

My Commission Expires: _____

[For Notary Seal or Stamp]

_____

NOTARY PUBLIC

Schedule A—Property Placed in Trust

All the grantor's interest in the following property: _____

_____

_____

_____

_____

_____

_____

_____

_____

_____

_____

_____

_____

_____

_____

_____

_____

_____

_____

_____

_____

Trusts

Cover Page

Living Trust (Married)

Of

_____

And

_____

Date Created: _____

Notes:

DECLARATION OF TRUST (Married)—LIVING TRUST

OF_____AND _____

This DECLARATION OF TRUST ("DECLARATION") creates a trust known as "The

_____and _____Living Trust", and is

entered into on this _____day of _____, 20____ ("TRUST").

1. **ESTABLISHMENT OF TRUST.** This Declaration creates a Trust between _____

   _____whose address is _____

   _____City _____,

   County _____, State _____

   ("WIFE"), and _____

   whose address is _____

   City _____, County _____,

   State _____ ("HUSBAND"), and collectively the Wife

   and Husband are the "GRANTORS" or "TRUSTEES".

   A. **CHOICE OF LAW.** The Trust will be governed by the laws of the State of

      _____, and all Trusts created by this Declaration, including

      Child's Trust, and actions taken by Trustee are governed under this State's laws,

      subject to the Trustee's fiduciary duty to the Grantors and beneficiaries.

   B. **SEVERABILITY.** If any provision of this Declaration of Trust is ruled

      unenforceable, the remaining provisions shall nevertheless remain in effect.

   C. **AMENDMENTS.** This Trust includes any provisions added by amendments.

2. **TRUST PROPERTY.** Grantors have transferred, or will transfer, to the Trustees, the

   property that may be added by either Grantors to any Trust in this Declaration including

   "**Schedule A**—Shared Property Placed in Trust," **Schedule B**—Wife's Separate Property

   Place in Trust" and "**Schedule C**—Husband's Separate Property Place in Trust."

   A. **AFTER-ACQUIRED PROPERTY.** Adding after-acquired property by either

      Grantor to any part of this Declaration is also permitted and will be used for the

      benefit of the Trust beneficiaries and will be administered and distributed by the

      Trustees in accordance with this Declaration.

B. ORIGINAL CHARACTER RETAINED. Until the death of either Grantor, property transferred to any part of this Trust will retain its original character as detailed in Section 3.B. If the Trust is revoked, the Trustee must distribute the Trust property to the Grantors based on the same ownership rights they had before the property was transferred to the Trust.

C. LEGEL AND BENEFICIAL OWNERS OF PROPERTY. Grantors are the legal and beneficial owner of all property in this Declaration and all property that may be added.

D. TRUST PROPERTY ADMINISTRATION.

    1)   **TERMINOLOGY.** The first Grantor to die will be called the "DECEASED SPOUSE," and the living Grantor shall be called the "SURVIVING SPOUSE."

    2)   **DEATH OF SPOUSE TRUST PROPERTY DIVISION DISTRIBUTION.**

        1. On the death of the Deceased Spouse, the Trustee will divide the Trust property listed on **Schedules A**, **B**, and **C** into two separate trusts, Trust 1 and Trust 2 according to Sections 2.D.2.2 and 2.D.2.3. The Trustee shall serve as Trustee of Trust 1 and Trust 2 (as defined in Sections 2.D.2.2 and 2.D.2.3.).

        2. "TRUST 1" will contain all the property in the Trust owned by the Deceased Spouse at the time it was transferred to the Trustee, plus shared ownership property with a total value equal to one-half of the total value at the time of the Deceased Spouse's death of shared ownership property, plus accumulated income, appreciation in value, and the like, attributable to the ownership interest of the Deceased Spouse, and his or her share of all property acquired in the Trust's or Trustees' names. Trust 1 becomes irrevocable at the death of the Deceased Spouse. The Trustee must distribute the property in Trust 1 to the beneficiaries named by the Deceased

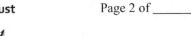

Spouse in Section 5, subject to any provision of this Declaration that creates a Child's Trusts or creates custodianships under the Uniform Transfers to Minors Act.

3. "TRUST 2" will contain all the property in the Trust owned by the Surviving Spouse at the time it was transferred to the Trust, plus accumulated income, appreciation in value, and the like attributable to the ownership interest of the Surviving Spouse and any Trust property left by the Deceased Spouse to the Surviving Spouse.

   a. Until the death of the Surviving Spouse, all rights to all income, profits, and control of property in Trust 2 will be retained by, or distributed to, the Surviving Spouse.

   b. The Surviving Spouse can amend or revoke Trust 2 at any time during their lifetime, without notifying any beneficiary.

   c. On Surviving Spouse's death, Trust 2 will become irrevocable, and the property in Trust 2 will be distributed to the beneficiaries listed in Section 5, subject to any provision of this Declaration that creates a Child's Trusts or creates custodianships under the Uniform Transfers to Minors Act.

4. The Trustee will have exclusive authority to determine the paperwork and record keeping necessary to establish Trust 1 and Trust 2.

5. Any Trust property left by the Deceased Spouse to the Surviving Spouse will remain in the Surviving Spouse's revocable Trust, Trust 2, without necessity of a formal transfer to that Trust.

3. **POWERS OF THE GRANTORS.** The Grantors have the powers deemed necessary and appropriate to administer this Trust, including powers granted by the State where this

Declaration is governed and is subject to the fiduciary duties to the Grantors and beneficiaries. The powers of this Declaration include, but are not limited to, the powers to:

A. AMEND OR REVOKE DECLARATION.

1) **BY GRANTORSS.** Either Grantor reserves the power to amend or revoke this Declaration at any time during Grantor's lifetime, without notifying any beneficiary, but must provide written notice to the other Grantor prior to making the amendment or revocation.

2) **BY OTHERS.** The right to amend or revoke this Declaration is personal to the Grantors, and a conservator, guardian, or anyone else may NOT exercise Grantors' power to amend or revoke this Declaration without the Grantors specifically granting the power in a separate Durable Power of Attorney.

B. RETAIN ALL RIGHTS TO TRUST PROPERTY.

1) **SCHEDULE A.** All rights to any income, profits, and control of the Trust property in **Schedule A** are retained by both of the Grantors until the death of both Grantors, and are shared property.

2) **SCHEDULE B.** All rights to any income, profits, and control of the Trust property in **Schedule B** are retained by the Wife, until the death of the Wife, and retain its character as being separate property of the Wife.

3) **SCHEDULE C.** All rights to any income, profits, and control of the Trust property in **Schedule C** are retained by the Husband, until the death of the Husband, and retain its character as being separate property of the Husband.

C. HOMESTEAD.
If the Grantors' principle residence is held in this Trust, Grantors have the right to possess and occupy the residence for Grantors' entire life, rent-free and without charge, except for taxes, insurance, maintenance, and related costs and expenses. This right is intended to give Grantors a beneficial interest in the property and to ensure that Grantors do not lose eligibility for any

State homestead tax exemption for which either Grantor may otherwise qualify.

D. **DEATH OR INCAPACITY OF EITHER GRANTOR.** If either Grantor dies or becomes incapacitated, physically or mentally, to where Grantor cannot manage this Trust, and whether or not a court has declared the Grantor incompetent or in need of conservator or guardian, the other spouse will serve as sole Trustee of all Trust, including any Child's Trust created under this Declaration.

E. **INCAPACITY OF BOTH GRANTORS.** The Successor Trustee must pay Trust income at least annually to, or for the benefit of, the Grantors and may also spend any amount of Trust income or Trust principal necessary, in the Successor Trustee's discretion, for the needs of the Grantors, until the Grantors, or either of them, are again able to manage their own affairs, or until their deaths. The determination of the Grantors' capacity to manage this Trust will be made by

_____,

who are reasonably available when the successor Trustee (or any of them, if two or more are named to serve together) requests their opinion. If a majority of these persons state, in writing, that in their opinion the Grantors are no longer reasonably capable of serving as Trustee, the successor Trustee will serve as Trustee.

F. **SIMULTANEOUS DEATH OF THE GRANTORS.** If both Grantors die simultaneously, or under such circumstances as to make it difficult or impossible to determine who predeceased the other, it will conclusively be presumed that both died at the same moment, and neither Grantor will be presumed to have survived the other, and the Trusts in this Declaration will become irrevocable. The Trustee will distribute the Trust property to the named beneficiaries.

4. **TRUSTEES.**

A. **TRUSTEES.** The Trustees are identified in Section 1. Establishment of Trust. Either Grantor may act as Trustee of any of the Trusts in this Declaration. The singular "Trustee" also includes the plural.

B. SUCCESSOR TRUSTEES. Upon the death or incapacity (as defined in Section 3.D. and Section 3.E.) of the surviving spouse, the "SUCCESSOR TRUSTEES" will be _____, and the Successor Trustees will become the Trustees at that time. If the Successor Trustees are not able to serve or continue serve as successor trustee, then the alternate Successor Trustees will be _____. Successor Trustees:

           _____ will have the complete and independent authority to act for and represent the Trust.

           [OR] [select only one]

           _____ must all consent, in writing, to any transaction involving the Trust or Trust property.

C. TRUSTEES' RESPONSIBILITY. The Trustees will serve as Trustees of all of the Trusts created in this Declaration, including any Child's Trust.

D. TRUSTEES RESIGNATION. Any Trustees may resign at any time by signing a notice of resignation and must deliver the notice of registration to the alternate Trustees under Section 4.B.

E. POWERS AND DUTIES.

    1)   **POWERS TO APPOINT SUCCESSOR TRUSTEES.** If the entire successor Trustees named in this Declaration, Section 4.B. cease to, or are unable to, serve as Trustees, any of the Trustees may appoint an additional Trustee or Successor Trustee to serve in the order nominated. The appointment must be made in writing, signed by the Trustees, and notarized.

    2)   **SPECIFIC DUTIES.** The Trustees' powers include, but are not limited to, the power to:

        1. sell Trust property, and borrow money and to encumber Trust property, including mortgage, deed by trust, or otherwise any Trust real estate.

2. manage Trust real estate as if the Trustees were the absolute owner, including the power to lease (even lease terms that extend beyond the period of the Trust), grant options to lease Trust real estate, make repairs or alterations, and to insure against loss.

3. sell or grant options for the sale or exchange of any Trust property, including stocks, bonds, debentures, and any other form of security or security account, at public or private sale for cash or credit.

4. invest Trust property in property of any kind, including, but not limited to, bonds, debentures, notes, mortgages, stocks, stock options, stock futures, and buying on margin.

5. receive additional property from any source and add to any Trust created by this Declaration.

6. employ and pay reasonable fees to accountants, lawyers, or investment experts for information or advice relating to the Trust.

7. deposit and hold Trust funds in both interest-bearing and non-interest-bearing accounts.

8. deposit funds in bank or other accounts insured or uninsured by the FDIC.

9. enter into electronic fund transfer or safe deposit arrangements with financial institutions.

10. continue any business of the Grantors.

11. institute or defend legal actions concerning the Trust or Grantors' affairs.

12. execute any document necessary to administer any Child's Trust created in this Declaration.

13. diversify investments, including authority to decide that some or

all of the Trust property need not produce income.

3)   **PAYMENT OF DEBTS AND TAXES.**

1. **WIFE.** The Wife's debts and death taxes are to be paid by the Trustees from the following Trust property: _____ _____.

   If the property is not sufficient to pay all of the Wife's debts and death taxes, then the Trustees must make a determination as to how such debts and death taxes will be paid from other Trust property.

2. **HUSBAND.** The Husband's debts and death taxes are to be paid by the Trustees from the following Trust property:_____ _____. If the property is not sufficient to pay all of the Husband's debts and death taxes, then the Trustees must make a determination as to how such debts and death taxes will be paid from other Trust property.

4)   **ACCOUNTING.** No accountings or similar reports are required by Trustees.

F. **NO TRUSTEES BOND REQUIRED.** No bond is required of any Trustees.

G. **NO TRUSTEES COMPENSATION.** No Trustees are to receive any compensation in any form for serving as Trustees, except that Trustees may be entitled to reasonable compensation, as determined by the Trustees, for serving as Trustees of a Child's Trust created by this Declaration, or for serving as Trustees if the Grantors are incapacitated.

H. **TRUSTEE LIABILITY.** With respect to the exercise or non-exercise of discretionary powers granted by this Declaration, the Trustee is not liable for actions taken in good faith.

5. **BENEFICIARIES.**

A.   **WIFE'S PRIMARY AND ALTERNATE BENEFICIARIES.** On the Wife's death, Trust property owned by Wife, as her share of the Trust property listed on

---

Schedule A and any separate property listed on Schedule B are to be distributed as specified to the beneficiaries named in this Section.

1) **WIFE'S SPECIFIC BENEFICIARIES.**

1. The property identified as _____

_____

_____

is left in Trust to_____

_____, the primary beneficiary. If the primary beneficiary does not survive Grantors or rejects the property, then to _____,

the alternate beneficiary.

2. The property identified as _____

_____

_____

is left in Trust to_____

_____, the primary beneficiary. If the primary beneficiary does not survive Grantors or rejects the property, then to _____,

the alternate beneficiary.

3. The property identified as _____

_____

_____

is left in Trust to_____

_____, the primary beneficiary. If the primary beneficiary does not survive Grantors or rejects the property, then to _____,

the alternate beneficiary.

B. **WIFE'S RESIDUARY BENEFICIARY.** The remainder of the property in **Schedule A** that is not assigned and validly disposed of in Section 6.A. will go to

("WIFE'S RESIDUARY BENEFICIARY") and if the Wife's Residuary Beneficiary does not take the property then to _____ _____will take the property as alternate Wife's Residuary Beneficiary.

C. HUSBAND'S PRIMARY AND ALTERNATE BENEFICIARIES. On the Husband's death, Trust property owned by Husband, as his share of the Trust property listed on **Schedule A** and any separate property listed on **Schedule C** are to be distributed as specified to the beneficiaries named in this Section.

    1)   **HUSBAND'S SPECIFIC BENEFICIARIES.**

    1. The property identified as _____ _____ _____

is left in Trust to_____ _____, the primary beneficiary. If the primary beneficiary does not survive Grantors or rejects the property, then to _____, the alternate beneficiary.

    2. The property identified as _____ _____ _____

is left in Trust to_____ _____, the primary beneficiary. If the primary beneficiary does not survive Grantors or rejects the property, then to _____, the alternate beneficiary.

    3. The property identified as _____ _____ _____

is left in Trust to_____

_____, the primary beneficiary.

If the primary beneficiary does not survive Grantors or rejects the

property, then to _____,

the alternate beneficiary.

D. HUSBAND'S RESIDUARY BENEFICIARY. The remainder of the property in

Schedule A that is not assigned and validly disposed of in Section 6.A. will go to

_____

("HUSBAND'S RESIDUARY BENEFICIARY") and if the Husband's Residuary

Beneficiary does not take the property then to _____

_____will take the property as alternate Husband's

Residuary Beneficiary.

6. **CHILD(REN)'S SUBTRUST(S).** All Trust property left to any of the minor or young

adult beneficiaries listed below in Section 6.A. will be retained in Trust for each named

child beneficiary in a separate Trust that can be identified and referred to by adding the

name of that Trust's beneficiary to the name of this Trust. The following terms apply to

each Child's Trust:

A. TRUST BENEFICIARIES AND AGE LIMITS. A Child's Trust ends when the

beneficiary of that Trust reaches the age of 35, except as otherwise specified in

this Section:

Trust for   Ends at Age

_____   _____

_____   _____

_____   _____

_____   _____

B. TRUSTEES POWERS AND DUTIES.

1) Until a Child's Trust ends, the Trustees may distribute or use assets for the benefit of the beneficiary as the Trustees deems necessary for the beneficiary's health, support, maintenance, or education. Education includes, but is not limited to, college, graduate, professional, and vocational studies, and reasonably related living expenses.

2) In deciding whether to make a distribution to the beneficiary, the Trustees may take into account the beneficiary's other income, resources, and sources of support.

3) Any Child's Trust income that is not distributed to a beneficiary by the Trustees will accumulate and add to the principal of the Trust for that beneficiary.

4) The Trustees of a Child's Trust are not required to make any accounting or report to the Trust beneficiary.

C. NO ASSIGNMENT OF BENEFICIARY INTEREST.
The interests of the beneficiary of a Child's Trust cannot be transferred by voluntary or involuntary assignment or by operation of law before actual receipt by the beneficiary. These interests are free from the claims of creditors and from attachments, execution, bankruptcy, or other legal process to the fullest extent permitted by law.

D. TRUSTEES COMPENSATION.
Any Trustees of a Child's Trust created under this Declaration will be entitled to reasonable compensation out of the Trust assets for ordinary and extraordinary services, and for all services in connection with the termination of any Trust.

E. TERMINATION.
A Child's Trust will end when any of the following events occur:

1) the beneficiary reaches the age specified in Section 6.A. If the Trust ends for this reason, the remaining principal and accumulated income of the Trust will be given outright to the beneficiary.

2)   the beneficiary dies. If the Trust ends for this reason, the Trust property will pass to the beneficiary's heirs.

3)   the Trustees distributes all Trust property under the provisions of this Declaration.

F. CUSTODIANSHIPS UNDER THE UNIFORM TRANSFERS TO MINORS ACT.

1)   All property that the minor beneficiary, _____, is entitled to under this Trust is given to _____ to act as custodian for the beneficiary under the State of _____ Uniform Transfers to Minors Act, until the beneficiary reaches the age _____.

2)   All property that the minor beneficiary, _____, is entitled to under this Trust is given to _____ to act as custodian for the beneficiary under the State of _____ Uniform Transfers to Minors Act, until the beneficiary reaches the age _____.

3)   All property that the minor beneficiary, _____, is entitled to under this Trust is given to _____ to act as custodian for the beneficiary under the State of _____ Uniform Transfers to Minors Act, until the beneficiary reaches the age _____.

4)   All property that the minor beneficiary, _____, is entitled to under this Trust is given to _____ to act as custodian for the beneficiary under the State of _____ Uniform Transfers to Minors Act, until the beneficiary reaches the age _____.

7. **CERTIFICATION BY GRANTORS.** I certify that I have read this Declaration and that it correctly states the terms and conditions under which the Trust property is to be held, managed, and disposed of by the Trustees, and I approve the Declaration.

_____   _____

Grantors and Trustees, Wife   Date

_____   _____

Grantors and Trustees, Husband   Date

NOTARY PUBLIC ACKNOWLEDGEMENT

The foregoing instrument was acknowledged, subscribed, and sworn to before me,

_____this _____day of _____, 20_____, personally known to me (or proved to me on the basis of satisfactory evidence) to be the person whose name is subscribed to the foregoing instrument, and acknowledged to me that he or she executed the same in his or her authorized capacity and that by his or her signature on the instrument, the person, or the entity upon behalf of which the person acted, executed the instrument.

Witness my hand and official seal.

_____

NOTARY PUBLIC for the State of _____

My Commission Expires: _____

[For Notary Seal or Stamp]

_____
NOTARY PUBLIC

Schedule A—Shared Property Placed in Trust

All the grantor's interest in the following property: _____

_____

_____

_____

_____

_____

_____

_____

_____

_____

_____

_____

_____

_____

_____

_____

_____

_____

_____

_____

_____

One entry per item.
Copy as needed.   **Declaration of Trust (Married)—Living Trust** Page _____ of _____

149

Schedule B—Wife's Separate Property Placed in Trust

All of Wife's interest in the following property: _____

_____

_____

_____

_____

_____

_____

_____

_____

_____

_____

_____

_____

_____

_____

_____

_____

_____

_____

_____

_____

_____

_____

One entry per item.   **Declaration of Trust (Married)—Living Trust**   Page _____ of _____
Copy as needed.

Schedule C—Husband's Separate Property Placed in Trust

All of Husband's interest in the following property: _____

_____

_____

_____

_____

_____

_____

_____

_____

_____

_____

_____

_____

_____

_____

_____

_____

_____

_____

_____

_____

One entry per item.
Copy as needed.   **Declaration of Trust (Married)—Living Trust**   Page _____ of _____

153

Trusts

Cover Page

AB Living Trust (Married)

Of

_____

And

_____

Date Created: _____

Notes:

DECLARATION OF TRUST (Married)—AB LIVING TRUST

OF_____AND _____

This DECLARATION OF TRUST ("DECLARATION") creates a trust known as The

_____and _____Living Trust, and is entered into on this _____

day of _____, 20_____("TRUST").

1. **ESTABLISHMENT OF TRUST.** This Declaration creates a Trust between _____

    _____whose address is _____

    _____City _____,

    County _____, State _____

    ("WIFE"), and _____

    whose address is _____

    City _____, County _____,

    State _____("HUSBAND"), and collectively the Wife

    and Husband are the "GRANTORS" or "TRUSTEES".

    A. **CHOICE OF LAW.** The Trust will be governed by the laws of the State of

        _____, and all Trusts created by this Declaration, including

        Trust A, Trust B, Child's Trust, and actions taken by Trustee are governed under

        this State's laws, subject to the Trustee's fiduciary duty to the Grantors and

        beneficiaries.

    B. **SEVERABILITY.** If any provision of this Declaration of Trust is ruled

        unenforceable, the remaining provisions shall nevertheless remain in effect.

    C. **AMENDMENTS.** This Trust includes any provisions added by amendments.

2. **TRUST PROPERTY.** Grantors have transferred, or will transfer, to the Trustees the

    property that may be added by either Grantors to any Trust in this Declaration including

    "**Schedule A**—Shared Property Placed in Trust," **Schedule B**—Wife's Separate Property

    Place in Trust" and "**Schedule C**—Husband's Separate Property Place in Trust."

    A. **AFTER-ACQUIRED PROPERTY.** Adding after-acquired property by either

        Grantor to any part of this Declaration is also permitted and will be used for the

        benefit of the Trust beneficiaries and will be administered and distributed by the

Trustees in accordance with this Declaration.

B. ORIGINAL CHARACTER RETAINED. Until the death of either Grantor, property transferred to any part of this Trust will retain its original character as detailed in Section 3.B. If the Trust is revoked, the Trustee must distribute the Trust property to the Grantors based on the same ownership rights they had before the property was transferred to the Trust.

C. LEGEL AND BENEFICIAL OWNERS OF PROPERTY. Grantors are the legal and beneficial owner of all property in this Declaration and all property that may be added.

3. **POWERS OF THE GRANTORS.** The Grantors have the powers deemed necessary and appropriate to administer this Trust, including powers granted by the State where this Declaration is governed and is subject to the fiduciary duties to the Grantors and beneficiaries. The powers of this Declaration include, but are not limited to, the powers to:

    A. AMEND OR REVOKE DECLARATION.

        1)   **BY GRANTORS.** Either Grantor reserves the power to amend or revoke this Trust at any time during Grantors' lifetime, without notifying any beneficiary, but must provide writing to the other Grantor prior to making the amendment or revocation, except as provided elsewhere in this Declaration. After the death of a spouse, the surviving spouse can amend their revocable living trust, Trust B, The Surviving Spouse's Trust, as defined in Section 6.A.3. and 6.B.3, and in Section 7.

        2)   **BY OTHERS.** The right to amend or revoke this Declaration is personal to the Grantors, and a conservator, guardian, or anyone else cannot exercise Grantors' power to amend or revoke this Declaration without the Grantors specifically granting the power in a separate Durable Power of Attorney.

    B. RETAIN ALL RIGHTS TO TRUST PROPERTY.

1) **SCHEDULE A.** All rights to any income, profits, and control of the Trust property in **Schedule A** are retained by both of the Grantors until the death of both Grantors, and are shared property.

2) **SCHEDULE B.** All rights to any income, profits, and control of the Trust property in **Schedule B** are retained by the Wife until the death of the Wife, and retain its character as being separate property of the Wife.

3) **SCHEDULE C.** All rights to any income, profits, and control of the Trust property in **Schedule C** are retained by the Husband until the death of the Husband, and retain its character as being separate property of the Husband.

C. **HOMESTEAD.** If the Grantors' principal residence is held in this Trust, Grantors have the right to possess and occupy the residence for Grantors' entire life, rent-free and without charge, except for taxes, insurance, maintenance, and related costs and expenses. This right is intended to give Grantors a beneficial interest in the property and to ensure that Grantors do not lose eligibility for any State homestead tax exemption for which either Grantor may otherwise qualify.

D. **DEATH OR INCAPACITY OF EITHER GRANTOR.** If either Grantor dies or becomes incapacitated, physically or mentally, to where Grantor cannot manage this Trust and whether or not a court has declared the Grantor incompetent or in need of conservator or guardian, the other spouse will serve as sole Trustee of all Trust, including any Child's Trust created under this Declaration.

E. **INCAPACITY OF BOTH GRANTORS.** The Successor Trustee must pay Trust income at least annually to, or for the benefit of, the Grantors and may also spend any amount of Trust income or Trust principal necessary, in the Successor Trustee's discretion, for the needs of the Grantors, until the Grantors, or either of them, are again able to manage their own affairs, or until their deaths. If both Grantors become physically or mentally incapacitated and are no longer able to manage this Trust, the person or persons named as Successor Trustee will serve as

Trustee. The determination of the Grantors' capacity to manage this Trust will be made by _____

_____,

who is/are reasonably available when the Successor Trustee (or any of them, if two or more are named to serve together) requests their opinion. If a majority of these persons state, in writing, that in their opinion the Grantors are no longer reasonably capable of serving as Trustee, the successor Trustee will serve as Trustee.

F. **INCAPACITY OF SURVIVING SPOUSE.** If, after the death of the Deceased Spouse, the Surviving Spouse becomes physically or mentally incapacitated and is no longer able to manage Trust B, the person or persons named as Successor Trustee will serve as Trustee.

   1)   The determination of the Grantor's capacity to manage the Trust will be made by _____,
   who is/are reasonably available when the Successor Trustee (or any of them, if two or more are named to serve together) requests their opinion. If a majority of these persons state, in writing, that in their opinion the Grantor is no longer reasonably capable of serving as Trustee, the successor Trustee will serve as Trustee.

   2)   The Successor Trustee will pay Trust income at least annually to or for the benefit of the Surviving Spouse and spend any amount of that Trust's principal necessary in the Successor Trustee's discretion, for the needs of the Surviving Spouse, until the Surviving Spouse is no longer incapacitated or death of the Surviving Spouse. Any income in excess of amounts spent for the benefit of the Surviving Spouse will be accumulated and added to the property of Trust B.

   3)   The Successor Trustee will manage Trust A, under the terms of this Declaration, until the Surviving Spouse is able to serve as Trustee of that Trust or until the death of the Surviving Spouse.

4)   The Successor Trustee will manage any operational child's Trust created by this Declaration.

G. **SIMULTANEOUS DEATH OF THE GRANTORS.** If both Grantors die simultaneously, or under such circumstances as to make it difficult or impossible to determine who predeceased the other, it will conclusively be presumed that both died at the same moment, and neither Grantor will be presumed to have survived the other, and the Trusts in this Declaration will become irrevocable. The Trustee will distribute the Trust property to the named beneficiaries.

4. **TRUSTEES.**

A. **TRUSTEES.** The Trustees are identified in Section 1. Establishment of Trust. Either Grantor may act as Trustee of any of the Trusts in this Declaration. The singular "Trustee" also includes the plural.

B. **SUCCESSOR TRUSTEES. Upon the death** or incapacity (as defined in Section 3.D. and Section 3.E.) of the surviving spouse, the "SUCCESSOR TRUSTEES" will be _____, and the Successor Trustees will become the Trustees at that time. If the Successor Trustees are not able to serve or continue serve as successor trustee, then the alternate Successor Trustees will be _____. Successor Trustees:

    _____   will have the complete and independent authority to act for and represent the Trust.

    [OR] [Select only one]

    _____   must all consent, in writing, to any transaction involving the Trust or Trust property.

C. **TRUSTEES' RESPONSIBILITY.** The Trustees will serve as Trustees of all of the Trusts created in this Declaration, including any Child's Trust.

D. **TRUSTEES RESIGNATION.** Any Trustees may resign at any time by signing a notice of resignation and must deliver the notice of registration to the alternate Trustees under Section 4.B.

E. POWERS AND DUTIES.

1) **POWERS TO APPOINT SUCCESSOR TRUSTEES.** If the entire successor Trustees named in this Declaration, Section 4.B. cease to, or are unable to, serve as Trustees, any Trustees may appoint an additional Trustees or Successor Trustees to serve in the order nominated. The appointment must be made in writing, signed by the Trustees, and notarized.

2) **SPECIFIC DUTIES.** The Trustees' powers include, but are not limited to, the power to:

1. sell Trust property, and borrow money and to encumber Trust property, including mortgage, deed by trust, or otherwise any Trust real estate.

2. manage Trust real estate as if the Trustees were the absolute owner, including the power to lease (even lease terms that extend beyond the period of the Trust), grant options to lease Trust real estate, make repairs or alterations, and to insure against loss.

3. sell or grant options for the sale or exchange of any Trust property, including stocks, bonds, debentures, and any other form of security or security account, at public or private sale for cash or credit.

4. invest Trust property in property of any kind, including, but not limited to, bonds, debentures, notes, mortgages, stocks, stock options, stock futures, and buying on margin.

5. receive additional property from any source and add to any Trust created by this Declaration.

6. employ and pay reasonable fees to accountants, lawyers, or investment experts for information or advice relating to the Trust.

7. deposit and hold Trust funds in both interest-bearing and non-interest-bearing accounts.

8. deposit funds in bank or other accounts insured or uninsured by the FDIC.

9. enter into electronic fund transfer or safe deposit arrangements with financial institutions.

10. continue any business of the Grantors.

11. institute or defend legal actions concerning the Trust or Grantors' affairs.

12. execute any document necessary to administer any Child's Trust created in this Declaration.

13. diversify investments, including authority to decide that some or all of the Trust property need not produce income.

3) **PAYMENT OF DEBTS AND TAXES.**

1. **WIFE.** The Wife's debts and death taxes are to be paid by the Trustees from the following Trust property: _____

    _____.

    If the property is not sufficient to pay all of the Wife's debts and death taxes, then the Trustees must make a determination as to how such debts and death taxes will be paid from other Trust property.

2. **HUSBAND.** The Husband's debts and death taxes are to be paid by the Trustees from the following Trust property: _____

    _____. If the property is not sufficient to pay all of the Husband's debts and death taxes, then the Trustees must make a determination as to how such debts and death taxes will be paid from other Trust property.

4) **ACCOUNTING.** No accountings or similar reports are required by Trustees for any Trust including Trust A and Trust B, except the final beneficiaries of Trust A and Trust B must be provided with copies of the annual Federal income tax return.

F. **NO TRUSTEES BOND REQUIRED.** No bond is required of any Trustees.

G. **NO TRUSTEES COMPENSATION.** No Trustees are to receive any compensation in any form for serving as Trustees, except that Trustees may be entitled to reasonable compensation, as determined by the Trustees, for serving as Trustees of a Child's Trust created by this Declaration, or for serving as Trustees if the Grantors are incapacitated.

H. **TRUSTEE LIABILITY.** With respect to the exercise or non-exercise of discretionary powers granted by this Declaration, the Trustee is not liable for actions taken in good faith.

5. **BENEFICIARIES.**

A. **WIFE'S PRIMARY AND ALTERNATE BENEFICIARIES.** On the Wife's death, Trust property owned by Wife, as her share of the Trust property listed on **Schedule A** and any separate property listed on **Schedule B** are to be distributed as specified to the beneficiaries named in this Section.

   1)   **WIFE'S SPECIFIC BENEFICIARIES.**

   1. The property identified as _____
   _____
   is left in Trust to_____
   _____, the primary beneficiary.
   If the primary beneficiary does not survive Grantors, or rejects the
   property, then to _____,
   the alternate beneficiary.

   2. The property identified as _____
   _____
   is left in Trust to_____
   _____, the primary beneficiary.
   If the primary beneficiary does not survive Grantors, or rejects the
   property, then to _____,
   the alternate beneficiary.

3. The property identified as _____

_____

is left in Trust to_____

_____, the primary beneficiary.

If the primary beneficiary does not survive Grantors, or rejects the

property, then to _____,

the alternate beneficiary.

B. HUSBAND'S PRIMARY AND ALTERNATE BENEFICIARIES. On the
Husband's death, Trust property owned by Husband, as his share of the Trust
property listed on **Schedule A** and any separate property listed on **Schedule C** are
to be distributed as specified to the beneficiaries named in this Section.

    1)   **HUSBAND'S SPECIFIC BENEFICIARIES.**

1. The property identified as _____

_____

is left in Trust to_____

_____, the primary beneficiary.

If the primary beneficiary does not survive Grantors, or rejects the

property, then to _____,

the alternate beneficiary.

2. The property identified as _____

_____

is left in Trust to_____

_____, the primary beneficiary.

If the primary beneficiary does not survive Grantors, or rejects the

property, then to _____,

the alternate beneficiary.

3. The property identified as _____

_____

is left in Trust to_____

_____, the primary beneficiary. If the primary beneficiary does not survive Grantors, or rejects the property, then to _____, the alternate beneficiary.

C. **REMAINING TRUST PROPERTY.** Except as provided by Section 5.A. or 5.B., all other Trust property of the Deceased Spouse will be transferred to, and administered as part of, Trust A, The Marital Life Estate Trust, defined in Section 6.

6. **CREATION OF TRUST A ON DEATH OF DEACEASED SPOUSE.**

   A. **TERMINOLOGY.**

   1) The first Grantor to die will be called the "DECEASED SPOUSE," and the living Grantor called the "SURVIVING SPOUSE."

   2) "TRUST PROPERTY OF THE DECEASED SPOUSE" will contain all the property in the Trust owned by the Deceased Spouse at the time it was transferred to the Trustee, plus shared ownership property with a total value equal to one-half of the total value at the time of the Deceased Spouse's death of shared ownership property, plus accumulated income, appreciation in value, and the like, attributable to the ownership interest of the Deceased Spouse, and his or her share of all property acquired in the Trust's or Trustees' names.

   3) "TRUST PROPERTY OF THE SURVIVING SPOUSE" will contain all the property in the Trust owned by the Surviving Spouse at the time it was transferred to the Trustee, plus shared ownership property with a total value equal to one-half of the total value at the time of the Deceased Spouse's death of shared ownership property, plus accumulated income, appreciation in value, and the like, attributable to the ownership interest of the Deceased Spouse, and his or her share of all property acquired in the Trust's or Trustees' names plus any property acquired under the terms of this Trust.

B. DEATH OF SPOUSE TRUST PROPERTY DIVISION DISTRIBUTION.

1) DISCLAIMER TRUST

_____ **NO DISCLAIMER TRUST** (Go to 6.C. Administration of Trust A.)

[OR] [select only one]

_____ **DISCLAIMER TRUST**, as follows:

1. After the death of the Deceased Spouse, the Trustee must divide the Trust assets into three shares, called the Survivor's Share, the Marital Deduction Share, and the Bypass Trust Share.

    a. **SURVIVOR'S SHARE.** This share consists of the Trust assets of the Surviving Spouse, as defined in Section 6.A.3. These assets will be held in and administered as part of Trust B, the Surviving Spouse's Trust.

    b. **MARITAL DEDUCTION SHARE.** This share consists of the assets that pass to the Surviving Spouse under this Declaration that are not disclaimed by the Surviving Spouse within nine months of the Deceased Spouse's death. These assets will be held in and administered as part of Trust B.

    c. **THE BYPASS TRUST SHARE.** This share consists of assets that pass to the Surviving Spouse under this Declaration that are disclaimed by the Surviving Spouse. The assets will be held and administered in Trust A, the Deceased Spouse's Trust.

2. **DISCLAIMER OF TRUST ASSETS.** The Surviving Spouse has the authority to disclaim any Trust assets left to him or her by the Deceased Spouse. The Surviving Spouse is not required to disclaim any of these Trust assets. If the Surviving Spouse chooses

to disclaim property, they will do so within nine months after the Deceased Spouse's death. Any disclaimed property will be called the "Bypass Trust Share," and will be held and administered in Trust A. If the Surviving Spouse does not disclaim any assets left to him or her by the Deceased Spouse's Trust, the Trustee shall not establish Trust A.

2) On the death of the Deceased Spouse, the Trustee will divide the Trust property listed on Schedules A, B, and C into two separate trusts, Trust A and Trust B.

3) All Trust property of the Deceased Spouse, as defined in Section 6.A.2., will be placed in a trust known as Trust A, after making any specific gifts provided for in Section 5.A. or 5.B., subject to any provision in this Declaration that creates child's trusts or creates custodianship under the Uniform Transfers to Minors Act.

4) The Trustee will place all Trust property of the Surviving Spouse, as defined in Section 6.A.3., in a trust known as Trust B (The Surviving Spouse's Trust).

5) Physical segregation of the property in any Trust is not required to divide that Trust's property into Trust A and Trust B. The Trustee will exclusively determine what records, documents, and actions are required to establish and maintain Trust A and Trust B.

C. ADMINISTRATION OF TRUST A. All property held in Trust A will be administered as follows:

1) Trust A becomes irrevocable at the death of the Deceased Spouse.

2) Trust A's life beneficiary is the Surviving Spouse.

3) If Wife is the Deceased Spouse, then the final beneficiaries of Trust A will be: _____

_____,

and the alternate final beneficiaries of Trust A will be: _____

_____.

4) If Husband is the Deceased Spouse, then the final beneficiaries of Trust A will be: _____

_____, and the alternate final beneficiaries of Trust A will be: _____

_____.

5) The Trustee will be entitled to reasonable compensation from assets of Trust A for services rendered managing Trust A, without court approval.

6) On the death of the life beneficiary, the Trustee must distribute the property of Trust A to the final beneficiary or beneficiaries, as named in Section 6.C.3 or 6.C.4.

7. **CREATION OF TRUST B THE SURVIVING SPOUSE'S TRUST. Upon the death** of the Deceased Spouse, all Trust property owned by the Surviving Spouse, as defined in Section 6.A.3., will be held in Trust B, The Surviving Spouse's Trust. Trust B will include any Trust property of the Deceased Spouse left to the Surviving Spouse and not disclaimed by them.

A. **ADMINISTRATION OF TRUST B.** Until the death of the Surviving Spouse, the Surviving Spouse retains all rights to all income, profits, and control of the property in Trust B. The Surviving Spouse may amend or revoke Trust B at any time during their lifetime, without notifying any beneficiary.

B. **DISTRIBUTION OF PROPERTY IN TRUST B.**

1) On the death of the Surviving Spouse, Trust B becomes irrevocable.

2) The Trustee will first distribute any Specific Gifts of the Surviving Spouse to the beneficiaries. The Trustee will then distribute all remaining property of Trust B to their final or alternate final beneficiaries.

3) All distributions regarding Trust B are subject to any provision in this Declaration that creates child's Trusts or creates custodianships under the Uniform Transfers to Minors Act.

8. **AMENDING AB TRUST WHEN ESTATE TAX LAWS CHANGE.** If the U.S. Congress changes the estate tax law, this Trust may be amended as follows:

   A. If both Grantors are alive, but one is incapacitated, the competent spouse may amend this AB Trust in order to take best advantage of the new tax law.

   B. If both Grantors are alive, but incapacitated, the Successor Trustee may amend this AB Trust in order to take best advantage of the new tax law.

9. **CHILD(REN)'S SUBTRUST(S).** All Trust property left to any of the minor or young adult beneficiaries listed below in Section 6.A. will be retained in Trust for each named child beneficiary in a separate Trust that can be identified and referred to by adding the name of that Trust's beneficiary to the name of this Trust. The following terms apply to each Child's Trust:

   A. **TRUST BENEFICIARIES AND AGE LIMITS.** A Child's Trust ends when the beneficiary of that Trust becomes 35, except as otherwise specified in this Section:

   Trust for   Ends at Age

   _____   _____

   _____   _____

   _____   _____

   B. **TRUSTEES POWERS AND DUTIES.**

   1)   Until a Child's Trust ends, the Trustees may distribute or use assets for the benefit of the beneficiary as the Trustees deems necessary for the beneficiary's health, support, maintenance, or education. Education includes, but is not limited to, college, graduate, professional, and vocational studies, and reasonably related living expenses.

   2)   In deciding whether to make a distribution to the beneficiary, the

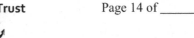

Trustees may take into account the beneficiary's other income, resources, and sources of support.

3)   Any Child's Trust income that is not distributed to a beneficiary by the Trustees will accumulate and add to the principal of the Trust for that beneficiary.

4)   The Trustees of a Child's Trust is not required to make any accounting or report to the Trust beneficiary.

C. **NO ASSIGNMENT OF BENEFICIARY INTEREST.** The interests of the beneficiary of a Child's Trust cannot be transferred by voluntary or involuntary assignment or by operation of law before actual receipt by the beneficiary. These interests are free from the claims of creditors and from attachments, execution, bankruptcy, or other legal process to the fullest extent permitted by law.

D. **TRUSTEES COMPENSATION.** Any Trustees of a Child's Trust created under this Declaration will be entitled to reasonable compensation out of the Trust assets for ordinary and extraordinary services, and for all services in connection with the termination of any Trust.

E. **TERMINATION.** A Child's Trust will end when any of the following events occur:

1)   the beneficiary reaches the age specified in Section 6.A. If the Trust ends for this reason, the remaining principal and accumulated income of the Trust will be given outright to the beneficiary.

2)   the beneficiary dies. If the Trust ends for this reason, the Trust property will pass to the beneficiary's heirs.

3)   the Trustees distribute all Trust property under the provisions of this Declaration.

F. **CUSTODIANSHIPS UNDER THE UNIFORM TRANSFERS TO MINORS ACT.**

1)   All property _____

beneficiary becomes entitled to under this Trust is given to _____

_____to act as custodian for _____

_____under the State of _____

_____Uniform Transfers to Minors Act, until the beneficiary reaches age

_____.

2)   All property _____,

beneficiary becomes entitled to under this Trust is given to _____

_____to act as custodian for _____

_____under the State of _____

_____Uniform Transfers to Minors Act, until the beneficiary reaches age

_____.

3)   All property _____,

beneficiary becomes entitled to under this Trust is given to _____

_____to act as custodian for _____

_____under the State of _____

_____Uniform Transfers to Minors Act, until the beneficiary reaches age

_____.

4)   All property _____,

beneficiary becomes entitled to under this Trust is given to _____

_____to act as custodian for _____

_____under the State of _____

_____Uniform Transfers to Minors Act, until the beneficiary reaches age

_____.

10. CERTIFICATION BY GRANTORS. I certify that I have read this Declaration and that
it correctly states the terms and conditions under which the Trust property is to be held,
managed, and disposed of by the Trustees, and I approve the Declaration.

_____   _____

Grantors and Trustees, Wife   Date

_____   _____

Grantors and Trustees, Husband   Date

NOTARY PUBLIC ACKNOWLEDGEMENT

The foregoing instrument was acknowledged, subscribed, and sworn to before me,

_____this _____day of _____, 20_____, personally known to me (or proved to me on the basis of satisfactory evidence) to be the person whose name is subscribed to the foregoing instrument, and acknowledged to me that he or she executed the same in his or her authorized capacity and that by his or her signature on the instrument, the person, or the entity upon behalf of which the person acted, executed the instrument.

Witness my hand and official seal.

_____

NOTARY PUBLIC for the State of _____

My Commission Expires: _____

[For Notary Seal or Stamp]

_____
NOTARY PUBLIC

Schedule A—Shared Property Placed in Trust

All the grantor's interest in the following property: _____

_____

_____

_____

_____

_____

_____

_____

_____

_____

_____

_____

_____

_____

_____

_____

_____

_____

_____

_____

_____

_____

_____

Schedule B—Wife's Separate Property Placed in Trust

All of Wife's interest in the following property: _____

_____

_____

_____

_____

_____

_____

_____

_____

_____

_____

_____

_____

_____

_____

_____

_____

_____

_____

_____

_____

_____

_____

Schedule C—Husband's Separate Property Placed in Trust

All of Husband's interest in the following property: _____

_____

_____

_____

_____

_____

_____

_____

_____

_____

_____

_____

_____

_____

_____

_____

_____

_____

_____

_____

_____

_____

_____

Trusts

Cover Page

Florida Witness Statement for Living Trusts

Of

_____

(And

_____)

Date Created: _____

Notes:

FLORIDA WITNESS STATEMENT FOR LIVING TRUSTS

On this _____ day of _____, 20____, _____

declared to me, the undersigned, under penalty of perjury that the person who signed or acknowledged the living trust was their living trust, called the Declaration of Trust dated _____ day of _____, 20_____, requested me to act as witness to their hand in signing the document in my presence, and did so in my presence. I sign my name being first duly sworn and do declare that the signatures of the Declaration of Trust mentioned above was signed willingly, or willingly directed by another to sign for him/her, and that I, sign below as witness and to the best of my knowledge all parties are eighteen years of age or older, of sound mind and under no constraint or undue influence.

_____   _____
Witness's Signature   Printed Name of Witness

_____
Address of Witness

Cover Page

Assignment of Property to a Living Trust

Of

_____

(And

_____)

Date Created: _____

Notes:

ASSIGNMENT OF PROPERTY TO A LIVING TRUST

I/We _____ and _____,

Grantor(s), and Trustee(s) of the Living Trust, dated _____, assign and

transfer all rights, title, and interest in the following property: _____

_____

_____

_____

_____

_____

_____

_____

_____

_____

_____

I/We execute this Assignment of Property on the _____ day of _____, 20____
and declare, under penalty of perjury of the law, that I am/we are signing and executing this
document willingly, under my/our own free and voluntary act, and that I am/we are of the age of
majority or otherwise legally empowered to make this document and under no constraint or
undue influence.

_____   _____
Grantor and Trustee Signature   Printed Name of Grantor and Trustee

_____
Address of Grantor and Trustee

_____   _____
Grantor and Trustee Signature   Printed Name of Grantor and Trustee

_____
Address of Grantor and Trustee

NOTARY PUBLIC ACKNOWLEDGEMENT

The foregoing instrument was acknowledged, subscribed, and sworn to before me,

_____this _____day of _____, 20____, personally known to me (or proved to me on the basis of satisfactory evidence) to be the person whose name is subscribed to the foregoing instrument, and acknowledged to me that he or she executed the same in his or her authorized capacity and that by his or her signature on the instrument, the person, or the entity upon behalf of which the person acted, executed the instrument.

Witness my hand and official seal.

_____

NOTARY PUBLIC for the State of _____

My Commission Expires: _____

[For Notary Seal or Stamp]

_____
NOTARY PUBLIC

Trusts

Cover Page

Affidavit of Assumption of Duties by Successor Trustee

Date Created: _____

Notes:

AFFIDAVIT OF ASSUMPTION OF DUTIES BY SUCCESSOR TRUSTEE

I, _____, Successor Trustee whose address is ____

_____City _____,

County_____, State _____, being of legal age

and first being duly sworn, declare:

On the ____day of _____, 20_____, Grantor(s) _____

and _____created a Living Trust with them as Grantor(s).

On the ____day of _____, 20_____, Grantor _____

died, and on the ____day of _____, 20_____, the other Grantor _____

_____died. A certified copy of the Certificate of Death is/are attached. The
Declaration of Trust creating the Living Trust provides that upon the death of the Grantors, I,

_____become the Trustee of the Trust.

I hereby accept the office of Trustee of the Trust, and I am from this time forward acting as
Trustee of the Trust.

Successor Trustee signature _____Date: _____

NOTARY PUBLIC ACKNOWLEDGEMENT

The foregoing instrument was acknowledged, subscribed, and sworn to before me,

_____this ____day of _____, 20____,

personally known to me (or proved to me on the basis of satisfactory evidence) to be the person
whose name is subscribed to the foregoing instrument, and acknowledged to me that they
executed the same in their authorized capacity and that by their signature on the instrument, the
person, or the entity upon behalf of which the person acted, executed the instrument. Witness my
hand and official seal.

NOTARY PUBLIC for the State of _____County of _____

My Commission Expires: _____

[For Notary Seal or Stamp]

Trusts

Cover Page

Living Trust Amendment

Of

.

_____

(And

_____)

Date Created: _____

Notes:

LIVING TRUST AMENDMENT

I/We _____ and _____,

as Grantor(s) and Trustee(s) of the Living Trust dated _____ make the following Amendments as allowed by the Living Trust:

1) Changes to the Living Trust: _____

_____

_____

_____

2) Add to the Living Trust: _____

_____

_____

_____

3) In all other respects we confirm and republish the Living Trust dated _____

as modified by this Amendment.

I/We subscribe to this Amendment this day _____ of _____, 20_____, and declare, under penalty of perjury of the law, that I/we sign and execute this document willingly, under my/our own free and voluntary act and that I am/we are of the age of majority or otherwise legally empowered to make this document and am/are under no constraint or undue influence.

_____   _____
Grantor and Trustee Signature   Printed Name of Grantor and Trustee

_____
Address of Grantor and Trustee

_____   _____
Grantor and Trustee Signature   Printed Name of Grantor and Trustee

_____
Address of Grantor and Trustee

NOTARY PUBLIC ACKNOWLEDGEMENT

The foregoing instrument was acknowledged, subscribed, and sworn to before me,

_____this _____day of _____, 20____, personally known to me (or proved to me on the basis of satisfactory evidence) to be the person whose name is subscribed to the foregoing instrument, and acknowledged to me that he or she executed the same in his or her authorized capacity and that by his or her signature on the instrument, the person, or the entity upon behalf of which the person acted, executed the instrument.

Witness my hand and official seal.

_____

NOTARY PUBLIC for the State of _____

My Commission Expires: _____

[For Notary Seal or Stamp]

_____
NOTARY PUBLIC

Trusts

Cover Page

Revocation of Living Trust

Of

_____

(And

_____)

Date Created: _____

Notes:

REVOCATION OF LIVING TRUST

I/We, _____, whose address is _____

_____ City_____

County _____State _____, revoke the Living Will

dated _____, in its entirety without limitations, including revoking any appointment of any persons named in the above Living Trust. Under the terms of the Living Trust, the Grantor(s) reserved the power to revoke the Trust. Under these terms, and the laws of the State of _____, the Grantor(s) revoke the Living Trust and state the Trust is completely revoked. All property of the Trust will be returned to the Grantor(s) and legally owned by the original Grantor(s) as defined in the Trust.

Grantor and Trustee signature: _____Date: _____

Grantor and Trustee signature: _____Date: _____

NOTARY PUBLIC ACKNOWLEDGEMENT

The foregoing instrument was acknowledged, subscribed, and sworn to before me,

_____this _____day of _____,

20_____,personally known to me (or proved to me on the basis of satisfactory evidence) to be the person whose name is subscribed to the foregoing instrument, and acknowledged to me that he or she executed the same in his or her authorized capacity and that by his or her signature on the instrument, the person, or the entity upon behalf of which the person acted, executed the instrument.

Witness my hand and official seal.

_____

NOTARY PUBLIC for the State of _____

My Commission Expires: _____

[For Notary Seal or Stamp]

_____
NOTARY PUBLIC

Appendix

STATE SPECIFIC INFORMATION

State Specific Information

Alabama:
PeerlessLegal.com/wtpo/al-alabama/
Alaska:
PeerlessLegal.com/wtpo/ak-alaska/
Arizona:
PeerlessLegal.com/wtpo/az-arizona/
Arkansas:
PeerlessLegal.com/wtpo/ar-arkansas/
California:
PeerlessLegal.com/wtpo/ca-california/
Colorado:
PeerlessLegal.com/wtpo/co-colorado/
Connecticut:
PeerlessLegal.com/wtpo/ct-connecticut/
Delaware:
PeerlessLegal.com/wtpo/de-delaware/
District of Columbia, Washington:
PeerlessLegal.com/wtpo/dc-washington/
Florida:
PeerlessLegal.com/wtpo/fl-florida/
Georgia:
PeerlessLegal.com/wtpo/ga-georgia/
Hawaii:
PeerlessLegal.com/wtpo/hi-hawaii/
Idaho:
PeerlessLegal.com/wtpo/id-idaho/
Illinois:
PeerlessLegal.com/wtpo/il-illinois/
Indiana:
PeerlessLegal.com/wtpo/in-indiana/
Iowa:
PeerlessLegal.com/wtpo/ia-iowa/
Kansas:
PeerlessLegal.com/wtpo/ks-kansas/
Kentucky:
PeerlessLegal.com/wtpo/ky-kentucky/
Louisiana:
PeerlessLegal.com/wtpo/la-louisiana/
Maine:
PeerlessLegal.com/wtpo/me-maine/

Maryland:
PeerlessLegal.com/wtpo/md-maryland/
Massachusetts:
PeerlessLegal.com/wtpo/ma-massachusetts/
Michigan:
PeerlessLegal.com/wtpo/mi-michigan/
Minnesota:
PeerlessLegal.com/wtpo/mn-minnesota/
Mississippi:
PeerlessLegal.com/wtpo/ms-mississippi/
Missouri:
PeerlessLegal.com/wtpo/mo-missouri/
Montana:
PeerlessLegal.com/wtpo/mt-montana/
Nebraska:
PeerlessLegal.com/wtpo/ne-nebraska/
Nevada:
PeerlessLegal.com/wtpo/nv-nevada/
New Hampshire:
PeerlessLegal.com/wtpo/nh-new-hampshire/
New Jersey:
PeerlessLegal.com/wtpo/nj-new-jersey/
New Mexico:
PeerlessLegal.com/wtpo/nm-new-mexico/
New York:
PeerlessLegal.com/wtpo/ny-new-york/
North Carolina:
PeerlessLegal.com/wtpo/nc-north-carolina/
North Dakota:
PeerlessLegal.com/wtpo/nd-north-dakota/
Ohio:
PeerlessLegal.com/wtpo/oh-ohio/
Oklahoma:
PeerlessLegal.com/wtpo/ok-oklahoma/
Oregon:
PeerlessLegal.com/wtpo/or-oregon/
Pennsylvania:
PeerlessLegal.com/wtpo/pa-pennsylvania/

Rhode Island:
PeerlessLegal.com/wtpo/ri-rhode-island/
South Carolina:
PeerlessLegal.com/wtpo/sc-south-carolina/
South Dakota:
PeerlessLegal.com/wtpo/sd-south-dakota/
Tennessee:
PeerlessLegal.com/wtpo/tn-tennessee/
Texas:
PeerlessLegal.com/wtpo/tx-texas/
Utah:
PeerlessLegal.com/wtpo/ut-utah/

Vermont:
PeerlessLegal.com/wtpo/vt-vermont/
Virginia:
PeerlessLegal.com/wtpo/va-virginia/
Washington (State):
PeerlessLegal.com/wtpo/wa-washington/
West Virginia:
PeerlessLegal.com/wtpo/wv-west-virginia/
Wisconsin:
PeerlessLegal.com/wtpo/wi-wisconsin/
Wyoming:
PeerlessLegal.com/wtpo/wy-wyoming/

Bestselling titles:

 Will, Trust, & Power of Attorney Creator and Estate Records Organizer: Legal Self-Help Guide

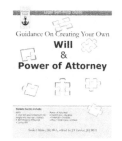 Guidance On Creating Your Own Will & Power of Attorney: Legal Self-Help Guide

 Simple Will Creator: Legal Self-Help Guide

 Give Through A Will & Living Trust: Legal Self-Help Guide

 8 Living Trust Forms: Legal Self-Help Guide

 Estate Planning in Plain-English: Legal Self-Help Guide

Made in the USA
Monee, IL
21 March 2024

55507071R00118